ANDA BRIVIN

GUN DOWN THE YOUNG

LIVING PORTRAITS OF AMERICAN ACADEMICS IN THE UNIVERSITY SETTING

SIMON & SCHUSTER CUSTOM PUBLISHING

Cover illustration by Raymond Majerski

Printed in the United States of America

10 9 8 7 6 5 4 3 2 1

This manuscript was supplied camera-ready by the author(s).

Please visit our website at www.sscp.com

ISBN 0-536-01460-4

BA 98333

SIMON & SCHUSTER CUSTOM PUBLISHING
160 Gould Street/Needham Heights, MA 02194
Simon & Schuster Education Group

"Sir, I would sooner counsel you to
gun down your young than send
them to an American university."

-- Simon Postle,
The Education of Martin Maguire, 1922

"All are punish'd."
-- William Shakespeare

Contents and Characters

Introduction

$\mathbf{A}$s one hard-boiled, pulp-hunting editor ruefully noted, this is not another tale of ghetto youth. In fact, on the surface, it is hardly about youth at all. What follows is humbly presented as an honest alternative to prevailing sentimental or irresponsible representations of life in American colleges and universities--more precisely, life among those individuals who control the educational community and oversee the processes by which the young are stripped of their childhood protections and prejudices and solemnly invested with the trappings and obligations of adulthood. Though naturally all of the characters portrayed in this series of vignettes are imaginary, there is a good chance that many will be recognizable to the late twentieth-century reader, in proportion as that reader is currently embarking upon, involved in, or has prolonged -- in memory or in more tangible ways -- a collegiate experience. For those who have been some time away from the campus, the following pages will provide an easy opportunity for updating outmoded ideas; for those preparing to undertake an affiliation with an American school, either in person, as a student or scholar, or at second hand, by sending forth both children and tuition checks, the work will serve as a warning, and help to offset some of the shock that accompanies all such transitions to alien modes of existence. In any case, a few basic definitions at this point may increase the reader's understanding and appreciation of the subsequent sketches.

The American university is characteristically divisible into two spheres, the Humanities and the Sciences. This is, of course, a gross over-simplification, as each broad category is composed of many altogether unrelated disciplines. Nor does this division take into account the many scholarly fields which combine or are outside of the realm of its two parts; the best example would be the law school, or the business school. Nevertheless, it is standard to describe the university in terms of these two, dominant entities, the Sciences and the Humanities.

In the Humanities, there is a general scholastic hierarchy, from the undergraduate to the graduate student (the latter sometimes serving as a teaching assistant), to junior and senior faculty members. In order for a junior faculty member to be guaranteed a permanent position at the college or university, he or she must earn tenure. The general context for teaching in the Humanities is the lecture, and, for more advanced courses, the smaller and more select seminar. Lectures and seminars are presented by all professors. After retiring, a distinguished professor will often be asked or allowed to remain on the faculty as a Professor Emeritus or Emerita.

In the Sciences, a similar hierarchy obtains, though there is perhaps a greater number of intermediary rungs on the ladder. This has to do with the physical tools and requirements of either sphere. Whereas scholars at every level of the Humanities work primarily with printed matter, and their movements are mainly, if not exclusively, circumscribed by the classroom and the library, it is the laboratory that is the focus of most of the scientist's activities. In the laboratory of a successful professor, there will be undergraduate interns, technicians, graduate students, and post-doctoral fellows. Of course some teaching is done in the lecture hall, but the real emphasis of faculty members in the sciences is the procuring of federal and private grant monies necessary for research. The tenure system, and the retention of retired professors, is the same in the Sciences as in the Humanities.

Finally, there is the administrative network of the university. The administration determines all policy, and ensures that it is carried out. Like the academic schools and departments under its control, the administration is hierarchical, comprising assistant and associate deans, full deans (many of whom also serve as vice presidents), a provost, a treasurer, and, at the top of the heap, the president. While responsibility for maintaining the educational philosophy and standards of the school is ideally shared by all members of the community, its success ultimately depends on the administrators and their decisions.

And now, having provided a general outline of the human architecture of the university, we can pass more confidently through the iron gates and into the lives of the individuals who toil and spin beneath its hallowed vaults, its gargoyle-crested gables, its chime-filled spires pointing like chalk-bearing fingers to the impenetrable blackboard of the sky.

Administrative Prelude

N o more funereal air prevailed at the obsequies of President Sleams than at the general administrative meeting held a week later in order to begin the process of his replacement. This overriding pall was due not merely to regret at the death of their colleague and principal, but also to the repugnance felt by all members of the upper echelons of the University to communal activity. In short, each of the twenty-five or so deans and associate deans and provosts and treasurers dreaded having his or her person -- and consequently, professional abilities -- exposed to the general view. Hence the predominant sorrow, the slow tread and somber bearing of the individuals who informally re-enacted their recent procession to the local cemetery. And though this time there was no casket in the high-ceilinged assembly hall named after the first President of the college, Elijah Root, there was noticeably more gloom and an even greater sense of loss.

Waiting in his chair at the head of the long oval table was the late Sleams's second-in-command, Dr. Raymond Pile, Vice President and Dean of Academic Affairs. The longer he sat, the lower his center of gravity seemed to sink. He was like a massive brie -- aged, creamy, puddling fast, oozing earnestness and sobriety from every tweed-covered, flaccid grey fold. When nearly all the seats were filled, he cleared his throat and made his first official proclamation to begin the meeting.

"You can serve the lunch now."

Like a swarm of bees or roaches, the catering staff appeared from out of thin air, hopping and buzzing about the table, filling glasses with white or red wine, piling plates with generous helpings of smoked turkey salad or thinly-sliced veal. The school escutcheon was pressed into each butter pat; there were tomatoes cut into the shape of roses, radishes cut into the shape of roses, and in the center of the table, a huge bouquet of lemon roses salvaged from the recent farewell service.

For some minutes, everyone ate in silence. When the noise of forks and knives striking china seemed to signal an end to the repast, a slim, ashen figure in matching outfit rose up before the board. Lyall Buttrey's complete lack of character and disinterest in all human affairs rendered him the closest to a non-denominational chaplain that the unofficially episcopalian University could withstand.

"Oh Lord of Heaven and Mother of Us All. For What We Are About to Receive..."

Everybody had seconds.

When the dessert plates were cleared away, the late President Sleams's secretary, a svelte, fortyish blond straight out of a Dawn Powell novel, stood up and, in her brisk, Brooklyn accent, called the meeting to order.

"Dean Poil would loik me to welcome awl of youse heah today, on this sad occasion. As you awl know, we at the college must begin owah search for a new president, since the passing of deeah President Sleams." And pronouncing the name of her late employer, with whom she had worked so closely for so many years, and whom she alone, outside of his family, had been privileged to call by his nickname, "Bunny," Velma Schwartz winced.

At this point, Denton Forrest, Dean of Graduate Studies, himself wincing at the sound of Velma's voice, stood up to ease the woman's painful burden, effectually taking control of the meeting.

"Thank you, Velma. We understand how difficult your situation must be. You can go now." Denton was still fuming over Ms. Schwartz's lengthy impromptu monologue at Sleams's funeral, something for which, to his mind, no precedent at this august institution could exist.

"As you know," he began again, but was immediately interrupted by Dan Wotsokades, far and away the fattest and most middle-aged in a room which seemed a convention of fat, middle-aged men. Dan was the pedophilic Dean of Student Affairs.

"I think, before we get carried away singing the praises of Sleams, we should all come clean and acknowledge that the man was a failure, both as a scholar and, more damagingly, as an administrator."

Dan and Denton, the only two men on their feet, locked horns silently across the table. Neither man had had the least respect for President Sleams, but for very different reasons: Denton, hired and rapidly advanced by the departed administrator, had equally rapidly acquired an intense and consuming sense of his mentor's inferiority, which is not at all rare among craven recipients of professional favors. Conversely, Sleams had always been prejudiced against Dan, and had once reprimanded the latter in resounding language for being caught in the act of taking photographs of select members of the Crew and Swimming Teams while they were showering at the gym. For which Dan had never forgiven the President. (In fact, if this were a mystery, rather than a series of true-to-life vignettes, these two Deans would be the prime suspects in what would surely have been the President's murder.)

Before either of the two men standing could launch his next missile, a third man slowly arose. This was Mr. Cuttle, one of a rare breed of so-called residual deans. The domain of his deanship had once been the Social Sciences, but since that entire school had been absorbed by the Humanities some fifteen years ago, Dean Cuttle had been left, like the father of the wife of Louis XV of France, without a country to govern, though he retained one of the loveliest offices on campus and, given his seniority, a staggering salary to match. At seventy-three, Cuttle was definitely the elder statesman of this cabal. Because he was by now old and generally incoherent, he was credited with great wisdom and integrity. After standing up, he seemed to have forgotten his planned comment and, after a pause, was forced to improvise in a mumble even more aleatory and confounding than usual. After another long pause, several of his colleagues applauded, and all three men sat down.

Seeing a golden opportunity in the confusion following Cuttle's ramblings, Sam Sertz, Dean of the Business School, made his presence known.

"I am sure we all appreciate the good intentions of our colleagues, Deans Forrest, Watsokolis and Cuttle, however, we have all come here to discuss the important business of keeping this University running. Consequently, I move to form a committee whose express purpose will be to choose the members of a Special Presidential Sertz -- I mean Search -- Committee."

In a unique moment of administrative harmony, all heads around the table nodded approval. In fact, the harmony was only superficial, as the members present fell into two distinct camps, those who took for granted that they would be appointed head of one or both of the new committees, and those who prayed that they would be allowed to play no part whatsoever in this affair.

Dean Sertz, whose joint appointment as Vice President for Budgetary and Grant Administration rendered him the most respected force in the room, continued his address.

"Therefore," he stated grandly, "because I have already been approached by several of you privately, I have decided to put aside my own overwhelming responsibilities in order to act as chairman of this committee."

Despite his declaration, no one in the room had actually solicited Dean Sertz's chairmanship of a committee which, after all, was only being formed now. But then, due to the utter lack of communications between any of the individuals present, no one could be absolutely certain that he or she was not the only person never to have sought out and made such a flattering suggestion to the Dean. Sertz knew and relied upon this absence of a synaptic network. But there was a woman whose way of thinking ran along the same lines as Sertz's. This woman knew that if Sertz successfully obtained the chairmanship of the committee responsible for forming a Presidential Search Committee, then he would stack this second committee -- of which his modesty would naturally prevent him from being a member -- with his supporters, who would subsequently recommend him for the post of ("Land sakes, it's a shock, but logical...") President. Though she had no aspirations to the presidency herself, at least not yet, she felt it her job to prevent the rise of Sertz, both in her capacity as Assistant Dean of Academic Affairs, and as a wife and mother, the former Mrs. Sertz. The usual little wave of awkwardness broke over the room when she stood up to speak.

"I applaud Dean Sertz's generosity, and second the motion to form a committee to elect a Presidential Search Committee. Furthermore, to maintain that spirit of generosity and open-mindedness for which Sam is rightly known," and here she winked at her ex-husband, exactly as she used to do before their messy lovemaking, "I would like to propose that we all vote on the members nominated to serve on both committees, and that we continue to follow tradition in giving priority to presidential candidates from outside the university."

Then the former Mrs. Sertz, smiling to right and left, sat down graciously.

If he had not already divorced her, Dean Sertz would have filed the papers then and there. The only thing that kept him from physically assaulting his former wife was the fear that an indictment would prove detrimental to his prospects in academia, though a soupçon of criminality was not necessarily an insurmountable obstacle to a successful career in education, judging from some of the things his colleagues had done to get where they were today. Why, he asked himself for the thousandth time, why had he dragged this woman up the ladder with him? And there she sat, thinking to herself that it was her pushing that had elevated them both. Dean Sertz groped for the arms of his chair, and returned to it, pale and slightly crumpled like a discarded memo.

The next pause was broken by intermittent whispers, such as, "Is wine the only beverage option?" and "Who was that blond woman? Is she coming back?" and "Good heavens! I thought Cuttle was dead." Finally one voice rose above the rest. It was that of little Spencer Bott, the Assistant Dean of Students, A through F, and worshipper of his boss, Miles Hardwick, Dean of Students, A through Z.

"Well, I'm sure that Miles would be perfect for that committee," proposed little Spencer, in a nasal whine resembling that of a flute clogged with spittle. Spencer was in fact a very musical man, playing the college organ at Sunday services in the chapel. Several of the older men assembled looked around; many of them were partially deaf, and seemed unable to trace little Spencer's piping to its source, a situation complicated by the fact that Spencer's head barely protruded above the gadrooned edge of the mahogany table. He was little, but perfectly round, and his low eyelevel was due to a combination of both substandard height and exaggerated girth.

"Who said that?!" hollered Dean Cuttle, seizing a rare moment of lucidity. But there was no time for a response, since Miles Hardwick simultaneously arose as though, like Napoleon in the *Sacre*, to crown himself emperor of the world.

"I second that emotion." The former Mrs. Sertz smiled whimsically, tossing another malicious wink in the general direction of her ex-husband. Dean Sertz acknowledged the second member of his committee with a resigned air and muttered back to his wife, through tightly clenched teeth, a threat to murder their children, who, fortunately for them, had already grown to an age at which their father could no longer be expected to recognize them.

One by one, nearly everyone in the room was nominated to the committee to form a committee to find a new President. Even those normally unwilling to take on extra work found themselves, roused by jealousy of rivals, insisting on being a part of such an important process, thereby rendering a separate committee superfluous.

In order to vent some of his increasing irritation, Dean Sertz raised another issue.

"Well, what about Dean Burber? As a Dean of one of the schools, his absence from this meeting makes it impossible for us to proceed." He grinned complacently, thinking he had foiled this subversive uprising against his bid for the Presidency. He was not prepared for the veritable riot which ensued.

"Milton Burber is a degenerate!" said the outraged Dean Hopkins.

"Though I agree with your assessment, how dare you use such a term?" rang out the sonorous voice of Paul Farnum, the half-Black, half-Hispanic homosexual whose combined personification of so many minorities made it unnecessary to provide the Office of Affirmative Action with a staff beyond Farnum himself.

Dean Forrest nearly climbed across the table in his earnest desire to convince everyone that Milton Burber was not only a degenerate, but dangerous. Naturally, Dean Wotsokades immediately took the absent man's side, at least up to a point, defending his importance in the theater world, but agreeing to his exclusion from all official university functions.

"Dean Burber is a much valued member of this community," said the Provost pacifically, proceeding to quote from various ambiguous reviews of the mysterious dean's campus productions.

"What exactly IS a provost?" questioned a younger assistant dean, far too loudly and non-sequentially.

Amid the growing clamor, a woman's scream was heard. For one moment people thought that President Sleams had returned. But no, it was only the very tardy Dean Burber, who arrived in a blaze of many-colored fabrics, with poor Ms. Schwartz using his entrance as a cover for her own re-admittance to the group. Burber's presence did not reduce the clamor, but merely fragmented and multiplied the topics of debate. At last the by-now-almost-entirely-liquid Dean Pile broke his long silence and joined the fray.

"Shall we have dessert?"

Chaplain Buttrey stood up to bless the dessert, but little Spencer Bott, who had been sitting under his elbow, poked him in the thigh and reminded him in a whisper that they had eaten dessert some time ago. For a moment, no one was standing, no one said a word.

And there they sat, heavy and brooding, like so many cannons set in place, defending an invisible fortress. But upon whom would they fire?

Oderint, dum metuant

Let them hate, so long as they fear

Max Stern

Full Professor, Department of Biochemistry

Adjunct Professor, School of Medicine

Salary: $108,000

H e knew he was right. About everything. If it could be said that he thought of any one thing, then that thing would be his own correctness. He scrutinized his barren office, for the only type of confirmation he needed, that which came from inanimate objects, from his professorial attributes. The stapler didn't disagree. Nor did the pencil sharpener, nor the desk pad. Even the configuration of the bean sprouts in his daily yogurt luncheon seemed to spell out recognition of the infallibility of his judgment, fresh bean sprouts being the nearest to a living interlocutor that he had known for some time.

Max Stern, M.D., Ph.D., pondered how he, with such a trail of abbreviations following his name, with memberships in such august scientific societies, and with such inarguable superiority in the handling of all matters, academic and otherwise, could have allowed himself to enter into an affiliation with such an individual as Sanjay Surat Ramani. It was not merely incongruous, but appeared to contradict all natural laws. Since he could think of no rational explanation, he decided to ascribe the anomaly to his innate and overwhelming generosity.

He thought back to his interview with Ramani, nine months before, and realized for the first time that he had been deceived by the young man's bearing and enthusiasm. He had had excellent luck in hiring Indian post-doctoral fellows in the past; they were usually extremely bright and eager, deferential, hard-working -- in short, terrified of being forced to return to their native country. They simultaneously saved the University money and shed an international glow over the departments to which they were invited. The only thing better would have been a *bona fide* Mexican female. But, Stern was forced to admit, Ramani had been the sole applicant.

A coffee-skinned, black-haired head bowed before the open door, and once again Max felt vaguely but comfortably like the Cary Grant character in *Gunga Din*. Despite the fact that he had requested the meeting, Max sighed impatiently, as a reminder to Ramani that the loss of his, Max's, time was a loss to the World of Science and Humanity.

"Yes, yes," he greeted Ramani. "Yes?" As usual, he allowed his visitor to initiate the conversation, in order that he might interrupt.

"Well, sir, you wanted --," Ramani began in one breath, with the staccato enunciation of Indians of his caste.

"The fact is, Sanjay, I mean Surat, that I have come to the decision that it is in your best interest that your time in this lab come to an end."

Ramani had a puzzled look. "Oh, sir, will this affect my salary?"

Now it was Max's turn to look puzzled, the novelty of which further irritated him. He rolled his eyes self-indulgently.

"I am afraid, as usual, you do not understand. Your appointment is being terminated. Your work here has been valuable, but your assistance is now superfluous. You --"

"Oh thank you sir. Does this mean I will now be making as much as Carmela in Dr. Reuther's lab?"

Max was finally forced to make what was for him an enormous concession. "Won't you sit down, Sanjay?" he offered, his exasperation thinly disguised. "What I'm saying may be difficult for you to comprehend. But it isn't really bad news. I simply feel that you have not been productive. In fact, you are holding back the lab. You must understand that I have a greater responsibility to science as a whole, a responsibility I have considered when I tell you that you are misguided in your career choice. I will of course be glad to recommend you for other post-doctoral positions, although I strongly encourage you to return to your home and rethink your future prospects and goals. In short, I think it more than fair of me to say that you are hopelessly underqualified for any jobs in the sciences in the United States."

Max's face never changed during this monologue, though at one point he did lean back in his chair and cross one pencil-thin leg over the other.

With the reference to India, Ramani was struck with the realization that this meeting was not going well. But the optimism which grows with fear pushed him to prolong the unpleasantness.

"Sir, if I am costing too much, you could maybe decrease my pay."

"Well, Surat, I'm afraid it isn't as simple as that. The fact is, an opportunity has arisen to employ a post-doctoral fellow with far better qualifications than yours. I am required to do what is best for this lab, the University, and the advancement of scientific thought. Consequently, Sur -- I mean Sanjay -- you will be given three months to situate yourself more appropriately." Max had begun to grow bored, looking about the room. His eyes alighted on a picture which, after a moment of study, he recognized as one of his two sons, taken when the boy was still in elementary school. He reached for the phone, as the standard and most convenient signal to the present time-gobbler that he was a very busy and important man.

"But sir -- " and, for one horrible, suspenseful moment, it looked as though Ramani was actually about to snatch up the receiver, if not Max's own hand.

Max looked intently at the Indian's confused and increasingly desperate face. As comfort was a skill he had never taken the time to cultivate, he began to feel awkward and wished that Ramani would, like the Hindu spirits he had heard of, assume a different form or simply disappear. Max stood up abruptly to end the awkward encounter.

"Well, as I am due at a meeting of the Committee on Academic Integrity...Remember, feel free to come to me if you require references..." Max led Ramani out the door like a sacred ox.

Having left his office an hour earlier than he had anticipated in order to extricate himself from the situation with Ramani, Max wandered aimlessly through the main courtyard of the science quadrangle, congratulating himself on his effectiveness as an administrator and his unwavering zeal in the quest for perfection among his staff. The sky was blue with, here and there, a suggestive cloud formation. The stone gargoyles poured approbation upon him. The last squirrels of autumn cleared the path at his approach. But to all of this Max was oblivious, his mind borne inward by the weight of loftier Ideas.

At 54, Max was at his intellectual and professional peak, or so it pleased him to think. Of course, an objective outsider, say a visiting scientist from a comparable university, might have been able to identify various signs suggesting the opposite was true. For example, the number of annual publications bearing his authorship had fallen off considerably in recent years. Those articles which had appeared had almost without exception been solicited on the strength of his former reputation. Even more disconcerting, his federal funding was consistently being decreased, hence this need for the constant shuffling of his personnel. Nevertheless, Max chose to interpret these symptoms as normal setbacks which always accompany the struggle for scientific greatness.

Max looked up to see, in the distance, Everett Morris, The Wilfrid F. Thrush Professor of Ancient History. It was Max's medical opinion that, despite his three wives, Professor Morris was homosexual, a fact which in no way detracted from the latter's prestige in his field, though it did allow Max a feeling of superiority for what he considered his colleague's frivolous interest in human affairs. The two men saluted one another, each feigning pleasure and mild shock at the unusual fortune that brought together people who had worked within yards of each other for nearly twenty years. Then Max, buoyant from seeing Morris looking less healthy than usual, and certainly less fit than himself, returned to the science building he had left only minutes before. There was still the possibility that he would bump into that Indian. So he entered the building furtively, but not altogether without the confident air befitting one of his stature, by the back door.

Two weeks later, the phone in Max's office rang, which provided him with the perfect excuse for dismissing a long-winded graduate student. It was a professor from The University of Texas, who wished to know Max's opinion of a recent applicant for a post-doctoral position there.

"I received your letter of recommendation concerning Dr. Ramani. When you describe him as 'extremely adequate' with 'a bubbly personality' do you mean this as a compliment?" queried the Texan caller.

"Not at all," responded Max, without blinking, though at the same time he reviewed in his mind the letter he had recently written for Sanjay. "Surat was something of a disappointment to me. He seemed incapable of grasping even the most elementary laboratory techniques. Also, and I hate to mention it, he has some problems communicating in English, though he swears it is his native language. I really think it would be best for him to return to India." Max paused to let the gravity of his pronouncements sink in.

"I am so glad that I called; your letter seemed ambiguous. Of course, I can't help wondering if Surjay is aware of how you feel."

"As a matter of fact, I have shown Sunrat -- I mean, of course, Dr. Ramani," (Max was a stickler for titles, however inferior those who bore them), "a copy of the letter and as far as I could judge he was highly pleased. He thanked me profusely."

The caller apologized for having disturbed Max, said that he would seriously consider his recommendation and hung up the phone.

Max sat back in his chair and reflected briefly on the conversation. For the first time, the possibility crossed his mind that his was not necessarily the most informed opinion of Ramani, that there might be others who had known him longer and had worked more closely with him, in fact, those far-away mentors who had originally recommended him to Max. They had said only that he was hard-working and, despite shyness, and a tendency to stammer when nervous, was willing to learn. Max had been deceived by their inability or unwillingness to state the truth. But perhaps he was now overcompensating for their error in judgment.

No. He knew he was right.

Si libenter crucem portas portabit te

If you bear the cross gladly, it will bear you

Ruthita Clabber-Jones

Full Professor, Chairman,

Department of Afro-Female Studies

Salary: $91,000

Ruthita Clabber-Jones combed the memo for slurs. She had not come to this college to be a racial watch-dog, but at this stage there was little else to do. When, ten years ago, the Department of Afro-Female Studies was founded, and she was called from the University of Alabama to be its chair, there had been plenty to do. In the first year, there had been over a hundred majors, but that number had now dwindled to eleven. Apparently, her vague premonitions were to prove accurate; Black Studies was merely a fad. When you came right down to it, young Black people really wanted to learn about white literature and Waspy Wall Street business techniques. And what Black women wanted, more than anything, was not to make a militant stand against their white and Black male oppressors, but to be made over in the mold of white Vassar graduates from the 1950's.

Ruthita glanced at the clock to see if it was time for her only appointment of the day. She was hiring her seventeenth secretary in ten years. All of her former assistants had been white women, with whom she had gotten along fine, at first. They had called each other "Girl" and "Girlfriend", they had shared lipsticks and lunches from white Styrofoam containers. But they had always, within weeks, grown apart, and Ruthita knew that it was her own fault as much as theirs, which is to say that she recognized the gaps which their different races rendered unbridgeable.

She was disappointed to find the memo on her desk free of glaring male- or white-oriented terminology:

To: All Faculty, Students and Staff
Re: Restroom availability
From: Dean Sertz

Due to an increasing number of unpleasant incidents, all restrooms, both men's and women's, will be locked by campus security at 11:30 PM, 5:00 PM on weekends. The only exceptions will be during sports events in the gymnasium. In order to enter and use the facilities after these times, you will have to contact the main security office at extension 999. They will dispatch an officer at their earliest convenience. Given the problems which this may cause, the Dean's office encourages you, if at all possible, to plan ahead and schedule your visits accordingly.

Thank you.

The Office of Dean Sertz

Well, thought Ruthita begrudgingly, we have come a long way since Blacks were forced to use separate bathrooms. But as this memo made no approving reference to those times, she had to content herself with the prospect of proving statistically that it took campus security far longer to respond to Black callers than to whites.

A bored Ruthita surveyed her office, which was one of the most expensively appointed on campus, a true showplace of Black Pride, Female Pride, and above all Black Female Pride. The walls were covered with masks and woven hangings produced by Ruthita's anonymous, impoverished Sisters back "home" in Africa, and the sofas and chairs were upholstered in inky Black leather. The floor was knee deep in white plush. There had been a stir when the redecoration was completed, some envious colleagues even suggesting that Ruthita had Blackmailed the administration into granting her such luxury. But it had always been an uphill climb for Ruthita. There was that time that Hannah Dartmouth had tried to do away with her. Only a law suit had reined the woman in. With regard to her office, the President himself had at last spoken in her defense. And so it was into her room-sized trophy for survival that, at five minutes past nine, Ruthita ushered the latest candidate for secretarial service.

Teesha Magruder stood nearly six feet tall, and though she was not fat, the size and tightness of her clothes gave one the impression that she was bursting out of them, leaving a great deal of her flesh exposed, with here a pucker, there a fold. If hired, she would be the first black secretary that Ruthita had even so much as interviewed, much less employed. Ruthita greeted her warmly as the young woman deferentially removed the stereo plugs from her ears.

"Well, I can tell from your résumé that you're an intelligent and hardworking girl," said Ruthita, in order to make it clear from the start that that was only half the battle.

"Thank you, Dr. Clabber," answered the girl.

"Actually, that's Clabber-Jones. Dr. Clabber-Jones. Jones is my ex-husband's name. But it's more mine than his. He got his name for nothing, but I had to work for it, so I kept it."

Ruthita was momentarily filled with nostalgia for the fierce battles of her married days.

"Are you married?" she went on.

Teesha seemed uncertain as to the correct response. In her confusion, she was unwittingly honest.

"Yes, Ma'am, I am."

"Happily?" asked Ruthita doubtfully.

"Yes. Very," replied the unsuspecting Teesha, again honestly. This was Ruthita's cue.

"Forgive my asking, but how is that possible? How can you, an intelligent Black woman, submit to the oppressive presence of a man who is allowed by tradition to consider you inferior? And our own men are worst of all! I'm assuming your husband is Black?"

Teesha felt strangely cornered. "Well, yes," she admitted.

After a pause, Ruthita smiled amiably and said, "Oh my dear, don't be so shy, I'm only provoking you, to see what you're made of.

Now, let's get down to more relevant issues. How do you fill your free time?"

Teesha was now utterly lost. "Well, ma'am, I don't have a whole lot of free time. I've got my three children to raise and the house to take care of. I help out at my church. My husband often works nights, so we all of us keep pretty busy."

"Three children, but you seem awfully young."

"I'm twenty-two," said Teesha, proudly.

"But certainly you have higher goals. Do you go to school? Do you belong to any Black organizations?" Ruthita continued to probe, having to remind herself that this was a Sister.

"Well, like I said, the church, and that's mostly Black," Teesha replied, and this time there was a pause before she added the "Ma'am."

The interview proceeded along these lines, with Ruthita more and more dismayed by the total apathy of her candidate -- her ignorance of the greater responsibilities of her Heritage -- and Teesha becoming almost belligerently defensive towards the end.

"Let's see," Ruthita said at last, standing up and extending her hand. "I think that will be all. I think I have a pretty good idea of who you are and I've certainly enjoyed meeting with you."

Teesha clutched the handbag in her lap with both hands and took a deep breath. When she rose to say good-bye her gold-colored bracelets jangled loudly. The two women gazed across a gap wider than any that Ruthita had yet faced, and then Teesha was gone.

Alone among her tribal treasures, Ruthita reviewed the applicant's résumé. It was impeccable. The girl could type over a hundred words per minute and had experience with nearly every sort of word processor. On paper she was ideal. If only there had been a trace of anger. If only she had shown that she had suffered. But in any case, when you came right down to it, Ruthita much preferred -- in fact, was only able to tolerate -- a bitchy, discontent woman with no true colors, just like herself.

Dulce et decorum est

Sweet and fitting it is

Lucretia Lopez-Vasquez

Full Professor,

Department of Microbiology

Salary: $81,000

Y ou have to be devious and manipulative to achieve this kind of greatness as a woman in the sciences. Lucretia Lopez-Vasquez admired herself in the myriad reflective surfaces of her lab. The hum of the stainless steel incubators and freezers was a comforting reminder that all was well with her cell cultures; they grew, divided and, ultimately, were laid to rest in their icy storage chambers. Even after fifteen years, she still felt thrilled at holding the power over life and death in her latex-covered hands. The smell of chocolate being eaten in some other laboratory on some other floor of the enormous building arrested her thoughts.

With a loud, satisfying snap, she removed the rubber gloves. Then she slipped out of her white lab coat and gently patted her professionally coifed, ash-blond hair. The aroma of chocolate presented her with a new challenge, and she knew from experience that she could not waste time. Her mind was already on the elevator, rifling through the possible locations where she might find the elusive object of her desire. She could rule out the sixth floor -- Max Stern ate nothing but rabbit food, which explained why he was the only man she knew completely lacking a torso. And the fourth floor was also out -- Harry Lang was a boring old diabetic. The fact that she was inconveniently situated between the two increased the urgency of her mission. She would try Reuther on ten because even if the chocolate were not his, he worked with *Drosophila* and there was bound to be some form of sugar readily available. Besides, Reuther could always be counted on to make at least a perfunctory proposition or flattering remark.

On the way up, her course was altered. A timid looking undergraduate, whom she vaguely recognized from her introductory course on bacterial replication, was standing before her snacking on a large Crackle-Crunch bar. With unabashed flirtatiousness, she bared her teeth in a girlish, effervescent grin.

"You may not have read the signs, but it is against the fire laws to bring chocolate into the building without offering me a bite."

The student first looked at Lucretia, then at his half-eaten bar of chocolate, and blushed nervously. He was unsure as to the expected response. He had only received a C+ in Professor Lopez-Vasquez's course, since which time he would have preferred not to meet her at all, much less to share his chocolate bar with her. But he was also a polite young man, and caught off-guard by her directness.

"Don't worry, dear, I'll only take a small piece," she purred, breaking off at least two-thirds of what remained.

Having gratified her gastric need, she did not get off on the tenth floor with her young supplier, but returned immediately to her own laboratory. There she found Hurami, one of her best teaching assistants. She could not recall whether he was Korean or Chinese. But he knew his bacteria, and she appreciated that.

Without preliminaries, he addressed her in amazingly fluent English. "I have just finished grading my exams, if you would like to look them over."

Lucretia swept past him, then perched languorously upon the corner of her desk. She smoothed her tight jeans, examining them for crumbs or flakes from the chocolate. She moistened her finger and quickly retrieved the few possibilities. Next, she checked each of her stiletto heels for potential damage, a gesture which was habitual with her.

"Well, Hurami, I was hoping to go to lunch soon. Would you like to join me? You could tell me how the exams turned out, and which students might not be up to par. And by the way, I just wanted to say that in your first month here you have more than proved your capabilities as a teaching assistant." By burying her request for his companionship behind a compliment to his teaching ability, Lucretia reduced the likelihood of the former being denied.

"Gosh, thank you. And lunch would be great," answered Hurami happily, as would any graduate student at what appeared to be the offer of a free meal.

"And you could tell me about the research experiences you had in your native country. I know, for instance, I would never have come so far in this field if I had remained in Mexico."

Hurami seemed flustered, but Lucretia was used to the confusion of foreign young men faced with such a glamorous and sophisticated personification of Female Intellect and Academic Success.

"Where are you from again?" she queried. "Refresh my memory."

"Hawaii?" he replied, every bit as interrogatively.

At lunch, Lucretia babbled on about everything but the exams. She was eating a meal of relatively modest proportions, in fact, more a breakfast than a midday repast: two fried eggs, a side order of bacon, several sausage links and a separate plate of hash browns. Hurami had a hamburger, no doubt to remind Professor Lopez-Vasquez of his American citizenship. After he had declined dessert, he watched his companion sample the chocolate ganache.

"This is such a treat for me," she explained, in between gulps, "I never eat chocolate at home." It did not occur to Lucretia that she rarely if ever ate a meal in either of her two houses, her own or the one she occasionally shared with her husband, a noted physician who lived and worked three states away. "And to think you can get such quality goods in the student dining halls! I'm very impressed." With that, she vacuumed the plate with her lips.

When the check arrived, Lucretia giggled.

"But really, are you sure you can afford this?" Now that Hurami turned out to be American, she had no qualms about letting him pay the bill.

The graduate student felt his left buttock, the muscle immediately behind his wallet, flinch. He was relieved to find that he had just enough cash to cover it.

Back in her laboratory, as hungry as though she had never left it, Lucretia was only half way through her perusal of the exams. She had already singled out two students whom she planned, based upon their performances, to abuse for the rest of the term, when she remembered that there was to be a departmental seminar that afternoon on a topic closely related to her own current research. It was being held by an untenured colleague, and therefore could not be missed. If there was one thing Lucretia loved, it was an opportunity to instruct less experienced and secure members of the faculty.

She arrived in the auditorium half an hour late, noisily helping herself to coffee and refreshments just inside the door. When, after another twenty minutes, it was time for the speaker to answer questions from the audience, Lucretia was the first to raise her hand.

"I think you must have failed to fully describe several important details regarding the bacteriological life-cycle. And, surely you are aware of the fascinating genetic manipulations which are now being performed in these organisms. You do not seem to be utilizing any of these promising tools in your own work," said Lucretia, swallowing loudly before making her point.

"Well, that was the focus of the first half of my presentation," replied the speaker, who had indeed seen her and groaned inwardly upon her dilatory arrival.

But Lucretia was not easily cowed. "Dr. Shrimpton," she resumed in a piercing tone, deliberately mispronouncing the name by shifting the accent to the final syllable, "you obviously have not acquired sufficient mastery of the topic if you are incapable of communicating your ideas successfully to **all** of your listeners!"

The speaker's exasperation was increasing, and increasingly visible. Meanwhile, Lucretia made a mental note to collect further information about this young man's prospects in the department. Other people began heading for the exits, providing the anxious speaker with an excuse for gathering together his materials and leaving the podium. Altogether unconscious that she had created the awkwardness which signaled the end of the seminar, Lucretia hastened to block his departure. The man smiled deferentially but not unambiguously at her and waited for her final remark.

"I am sorry to say that you will never accomplish anything in this field if you fail to appreciate the advice of your considerably more experienced employers." And her breath stank of donuts and her teeth were coffee-stained.

De Profundis

From the depths

Compton Swallow

Distinguished Poet-In-Residence,

Visiting Adjunct Professor,

Department of English Literature

Salary: $85,000

Lights glittered in the great chandelier and a fire roared in the grate. Stacks of cucumber sandwiches and blocks of odorous cheeses were passed from the kitchen by hired and properly attired graduate students who cared little for poetry but needed the extra cash. Professor Polyps's wife had even lent her maid to oversee the preparation of the meringues. Crystal decanters filled with rubiginous liquids were carried in on old, commemorative silver trays. The Spode plates, depicting views of the original campus, shone in glass-doored breakfronts and the gold-edged brocades were drawn over the windows to advertise the exclusivity of the function being held inside.

For the Miltonians, it was the climactic evening of the fall term. Since the founding of this most august, undergraduate literary society, by Ozias Barkley in 1820, the members had met on the night of the full moon in November in order to drink deep from the wells of Bacchus and Apollo. Barkley himself had been only a third-rate pen-pusher and fanatical imitator of the author of *Paradise Lost*, but with the founding of this society his place in history was secured. The little wooden house in which he had lived was still the club's center of activity; his bedroom, down to the chamber pot and the nightcap hanging from his four-poster bed, was preserved exactly as he had left it when he died.

It had long since been the tradition of the Miltonians to invite the university's annual Distinguished Poet-in-Residence (as opposed to the many undistinguished and unofficial claimants to the title) to give a reading of his works and then to celebrate his accomplishments with an orgy, not of gluttony and sex, but of well-timed quips and delicate finger foods. And no greater Star in the Literary Heavens had ever graced these rooms than the guest scheduled for tonight, Compton Swallow.

The university had been trying to tempt Mr. Swallow with the honor of being Distinguished Poet-in-Residence for many years. It was only following his stroke, the previous May, that he had decided to take up the position, though this was the first year he had not been asked. Stroke or no stroke, he was still the most prolific poet surviving from the generation just after Eliot, Pound and Yeats, with each of whom he claimed to have been intimate, and each of whose deaths he had celebrated in a lengthy elegy rich in ambiguous metaphor and privately printed and bound.

Diotima Maxwell -- Dixie to her friends, of which her family name and fortune guaranteed her a considerable supply -- was the Treasurer and unofficial public relations manager for the Miltonians. A chubby blond senior whose spectacles seemed stretched to breaking point by her head, Dixie lived for literature. And she was also an aspiring poet in her own right, her verse resembling now the tortured, suicidal monologues of Sylvia Plath, now the sentimental romantic reveries of Sarah Teasdale. As Dixie had admired him from afar for years, at one point even forcing her parents to purchase a summer home near Mr. Swallow's on Long Island, she appointed herself to approach the Distinguished Man, in order to explain the traditions of the Miltonians and to invite him to fulfill his duty and assume his position among their pantheon.

When, two weeks before the big night, she entered Mr. Swallow's office, she had a clearer view of him than she had ever obtained on the beach with high-powered binoculars. And she was somewhat startled at such close range. The man before her was large and slovenly, with an aura of more than the standard, deliberate academic shabbiness about him. There was also the distinct smell of long-digested -- which is to say, no longer identifiable -- foodstuffs clinging to the faded velvet jacket, though clues to these forgotten meals could be found along the cuffs and frayed lapels.

So this was her idol! thought Dixie, straining to hide her growing disillusionment. These were the cracked and dry lips that had whispered comfort to the dying Wallace Stevens. These were the grimy hands that had written some of her favorite lines in the English language; she thought of the famous passage in which Swallow spoke metaphorically of "the muddy puddles of our godless days" -- it had never crossed Dixie's mind that he had actually played in them.

Summoning all of the good-natured grace that she had learned to feign at finishing school, Dixie finally brought herself to invite Mr. Swallow to the annual Miltonian ritual. For a brief moment, she prayed that he would be forced to decline; she even suggested that if his health were to prevent his attendance, the Miltonians would certainly understand. After all, she thought to herself, she would gladly sacrifice two centuries of tradition rather than risk the public display of such a character, one whose greatest and loudest fan she was well known to be. But Mr. Swallow accepted the invitation with alacrity, sputtering out his thanks with particles of his most recent meal. With a heavy heart, Dixie left his office, but not before reminding him diplomatically that the event was extremely formal, and called for an elegant -- and, she was tempted to add, clean -- suit of clothes.

How relieved Dixie was when at last Mr. Swallow arrived, dressed with exquisite taste in a dark suit by Lubin, with polished shoes and an Hermes tie. She continued, her nervousness diminishing, to follow him with her eyes as he made a slow tour of the rooms, speaking in soft tones to the undergraduates and members of the faculty who swarmed about him, pausing to sip his claret or swallow a cheese puff with the delicacy of a duchess in the pages of Proust or St. Simon. At last, it was time for him to read.

When all the members and their guests were seated in the long-windowed drawing room, Marty Fellows, this year's president of the society, stood up to introduce the Distinguished Poet.

"Welcome, everybody, to a most special meeting of the Miltonian Society. In the spirit of our namesake, whose monumental works, such as *Paradise Lost* and ... many other poems, will live forever in history, we bring to you tonight a sampling of the immortal achievement of one of this country's greatest living poets, read by himself. Ladies and Gentlemen, I give you Mr. Compton Swallow."

Amidst enthusiastic but discreet applause, Compton arose, took one last sip of claret and moved to the podium. What a refined figure he cut, thought Dixie, once again proud of her famous literary icon. A hush descended on the crowd and there were tears in Dixie's eyes when the poet read the first line of what was surely the most tender and beautiful of all his youthful sonnets.

"Oh, bud of summer, share with me thy sap."

The line was left dangling, followed by a pause of the sort which commonly precedes large-scale natural disasters. Dixie tugged once, nervously, at the bosom of her strapless gown.

"Brrrwooooaaaahhhhh!"

Compton erupted with an earth-shattering belch. The sherry shook in the glasses. Dixie wanted to die. And, upstairs, Ozias roared in his bed.

Gaudeamus igitur

Let us then rejoice

Michael Shrimpton

Assistant Professor,

Department of Microbiology

Salary: $62,000

Dr. Michael Shrimpton, Assistant Professor of Microbiology, shuffled his papers together and shoved them into his Genuine Calfskin briefcase. All of a sudden he realized that he was alone in his laboratory, and had been for some time. Glancing at the clock, he found it difficult to believe that six hours had passed since his seminar had ended. So, with the mystery he had been reading tucked under his arm, he turned off the lights and headed out of the building to his car. On the way, he reviewed the day's events and made a prioritized list of the things that still remained to be done before his trip next week.

He had the car started and was pulling out of the faculty parking lot when he first considered where he had to go. It was a quarter past eleven. Suddenly he remembered his wife, not anything particular about her, only that he had one. Since she was in the habit of having dinner ready by seven, she would no doubt accuse him of being late, as usual. And of course her natural testiness at his lack of punctuality would be aggravated by the fact that she was two weeks overdue.

Recalling first his wife, then her condition, reminded him that he must get in touch with Dr. Stiffley at the University Hospital. If he could convince Stiffley to induce labor this Saturday, as opposed to Monday morning as planned, then he would be able to catch up on all of his professional correspondence before leaving for his trip to California on Monday. Moreover, if he could convince his friend, Dr.

Jenkins, the head of Labor and Delivery, to keep his wife hospitalized until the following Monday, he would not have to shorten his trip in order to bring her home.

Ah. But what about Bobby? After recalling his wife and her condition, the image of his two-year-old son toddled into his brain. Bobby would certainly need someone to look after him. But no doubt his wife had already arranged for that. Relieved, as though he himself had successfully delivered the new child and seen to the care and well-being of his three dependents, his mind shifted to more pressing matters.

His seminar had gone well, indeed, very well. The ill-timed and distracting arrival of that Lucretia Vasquez-Lopez had hardly dimmed the brilliance of his presentation. He had met with reporters from three different scientific newsletters about his latest contributions to the field. His picture was taken during two of these interviews, which reminded him to be sure and have his wife launder all of his shirts before being admitted.

To the hospital.

Her condition.

The dog!

The car swerved and sideswiped the curb. He had completely forgotten about Marie (named, of course, after Madame Curie), and since his wife had, during one of her understandable testy spells, forced him to accept responsibility for his own sheepdog during the gestation period -- his wife's gestation period, not the dog's, she had been spayed -- he now had to find someone to take care of her while the family was away. Unless perhaps whoever was going to take care of Bobby could be convinced that the boy would need his dog while his mother was in the hospital. At least Michael could propose this logical solution to his wife, assuming that she had already found someone to take care of Bobby.

The neon sign at the local all-night grocery store reminded him that he had promised his wife that he would bring home ... something ... he couldn't remember exactly what. He crossed three lanes of traffic without signaling and pulled into the parking lot. Perhaps he would remember what he was expected to bring home once he was inside. At the very least, the stop would provide him with another excuse for his tardiness.

In the midst of formulating a new method for fermenting *E. coli*, he was struck by a package of frozen tamales. Not literally, of course. But there was something about the stacks of frozen Mexican food items that jarred his memory. He knew that the one thing his wife had definitely not asked him to bring home was frozen Mexican food. Nevertheless, he himself was suddenly aware of a violent appetite for these tamales. Perhaps this had something to do with Professor Vasquez-Lopez.

He browsed through the next few aisles, thinking of which software he should purchase for his new Personal Computer, then trying to balance his laboratory budget in his mind, and finally considering how best to obtain more power in the department, thereby lessening his teaching load and increasing his attendance at conferences. This train of reflections led him to the dairy section and a more detailed agenda for his journey on Monday. Distractedly piling two full gallons of milk into a cart which, embarrassingly, turned out to belong to a little old Chinese lady, he decided that it would be best to attend the workshop organized by his co-worker, Dr. Reuther, but to forego the seminar by the well-known but limited Sandra Shore, a colleague from a lesser university and also a lesser, former girlfriend. Besides, Reuther's workshop was sure to be popular with younger females in the field and that always made being away from home easier and more relaxing.

By the time he got to the checkout, his grocery cart was overflowing with the most diverse selections, many of which he would not recall having made later on. There were the tamales and the two cartons of milk, a large wedge of the best Brie he could find, lightbulbs, multiple boxes of pasta, razor blades, crumpets, jelly beans, domestic vegetables and exotic fruits. No one of them could definitely be said to be The Thing which his wife had requested and even written down for him on a piece of paper he would not find for weeks to come. But surely she would be overwhelmed by the abundant proofs of his consideration for her, even if, in buying these things, he had consulted only his own appetites and needs.

The time on the sales receipt said "12:35 AM". He sped his Honda down the street and into his driveway. No lights were on when he entered his home, tripping over Marie and crushing one of Bobby's mechanical toys. It took several trips, and several breakages, to unload the car. After popping his frozen Mexican meal into the microwave, he was startled to see a strange woman, in housecoat and fluffy slippers, approaching from the darkness of the living room.

"You've been to the hospital, then?" his mother-in-law inquired, beaming at him.

He had completely forgotten about her arrival two days before. He automatically crossed out the names "Bobby" and "Marie" from the memo pad in his mind.

"Not at all, why?" he responded, with the slight, irrepressible irritation of the overworked male. His mother-in-law looked abashed, but she had always been a bit distracted.

"Well," she began, hesitantly, "You have a new little girl. Didn't you get the messages?"

"How wonderful," he said, with real feeling. And his mother-in-law assumed that he was referring to the successful delivery of his new offspring, but that was not it at all.

This was better than he had dared to hope. Now he could work all day tomorrow in his lab, finish his correspondence on Sunday and the mystery on the plane. And he wouldn't have to shorten his trip. The only thing he regretted was having wasted so much time worrying about it. For this he vaguely blamed his wife, though he would never have said so. With her in her present condition.

Dux femina facti

The leader of the enterprise a woman

Hannah Dartmouth

Full Professor,

Department of Comparative Literature

Salary: $103,000

From a distance, she might be your grandmother, or anybody's grandmother. As she approaches, you can see the wide, grandmotherly smile, and smell the tea-rose *eau de cologne*, and pity somewhat the stooping posture and the massive form, the precise outline of which can only be guessed at and seems constantly to change beneath billowing lengths of flower-patterned fabric. When she enters a room, it is like the delivery of an awkwardly large sofa, but one which is bound to prove comfortable and enduring.

And then one day, at a reception or seminar or some other campus function, you find yourself closer to her, and have the opportunity to examine her in greater detail. You note from behind that it has been some time since the wiry filaments of her iron gray hair have been dyed orange, and this might even enhance the sympathy you feel for the old woman, as she teeters lopsidedly under the weight of her enormous handbag, giving her the appearance of a good-natured hunchback or a bloated but friendly dowager from the time of Catherine the Great. When she turns around to meet you, you are struck by the soft, welcoming folds of her flaccid face, and just when you are about to throw your arms around her as if she were your long dead Great Aunt Gertie, the one who always filled you up with chocolate cake, she speaks.

All familial thoughts are abruptly driven away, and you find yourself wriggling beneath her dissecting gaze. The idea that she is assessing your potential nutritional value to herself and her allies marks the abrupt end to your pleasant reminiscences. You think to yourself, "She knows that I have my underwear on inside out." And, if you are a man, you feel that she has already castrated you in her mind.

It has taken Hannah Dartmouth years to invent and attain the position of Supreme Defender of the Female Intellect, an honor she now guards tenaciously and all others respect, at this university and throughout the English-speaking world. A female Moses expostulating from the mountain top, among the growing tribes of women scholars, her word is Law.

"Do I understand that you actually intend to support Ms. Severini's application for tenure at this university?" Professor Dartmouth is aggressively perplexed.

Still paralyzed under her pin-like stare, you find yourself unable to respond to this question, which apparently suits her just fine, as she has no real interest in your opinion, except as it can be restructured to resemble her own.

"Because before you do, I think you should know certain facts about Ms. Severini which have, typically, been played down by the male-dominated administration."

The Ms. Severini in question is the third female member of Professor Dartmouth's department to come up for tenure in four years. The other two, despite their impressive qualifications and widespread support from other colleagues, have been denied in their bids, due above all to Hannah's vigorous campaigns against them. But Ms. Severini is even more obviously deserving than her two predecessors and, furthermore, the Comparative Literature Department has been severely short-handed since the deaths or departures of three other tenured professors in as many years. Hannah Dartmouth, however, is altogether invulnerable to such sentimental arguments.

It may seem a paradox that the woman who, in her own mind and in the minds of many Amazonian devotees, has done more to further the cause of female scholarship and to advance the power of the feminine presence in academia, is consistently found to have deep-seated, negative reactions to colleagues of her own gender. Comments to this effect have more than once been heard to fall from whispering male lips at faculty picnics, where the open spaces allow greater distance from the ever-present Professor Dartmouth than the closed quarters of the faculty lounge provide. Of course, Hannah herself is perfectly aware of this interpretation, and brushes it off coquettishly as another example of masculine vindictiveness.

"For instance," Professor Dartmouth continues, with no intention of providing you with arbitrary examples but rather of drilling you with all of the ammunition available from her arsenal of professional contempt, "Severini has consistently refused to refuse to support the hiring of male technicians in the language lab, a strange attitude for a modern woman to assume, I'm sure you will agree. Furthermore, she recently told one of my most promising graduate students, Goneril McGrew, that the latter would not be allowed to register for her course dealing with women in German cinema, or some such new-fangled nonsense, on the feeble pretext that Goneril had missed the first eleven lectures and that the class was already over-filled." Hannah's acknowledgment that her younger colleague's course might be very popular would be purely accidental, and she would immediately attempt to reverse the implication.

Fear that any movement, much less verbal contradiction, on your part will only drive her pins in deeper, you smile and long for someone courageous to interrupt, but this rarely if ever happens; when you are near Hannah, you are entirely her own.

"Finally, and most disturbing of all, Severini has failed to show any enthusiasm for the most original and potentially the most significant contribution to the Humanities ever conceived at this university. I am speaking, as you must know, of the Committee on Femineutics, a field which I myself have defined and plan to establish as a separate curriculum."

You are afraid even to blink. You vaguely remember having heard the term 'femineutics' before, but never until now have you heard it used in a serious context. The sweat begins to trickle down your spine, and the widening of Hannah's eyes makes you wonder if she senses this minute increase in the local humidity.

"Have you ever noticed the way she pretends to be stupid when tenured male faculty are around?" She is now raising her voice. "And the way she dresses! You must admit that she is altogether unsuitable for employment here. All things considered, one must question how she acquired those honors that she claims to have received."

As her agitation increases, you find yourself wondering whether she actually uses the knitting needles sticking out of her enormous bag. It is more and more difficult to imagine her in anything like a domestic setting. Is it true that she was beautiful when she was young? Is it possible that she spent a night with Sartre, and to this day considers herself as having been the love of his life, making loud shows of irritation and embarrassment at the mention of Simone de Beauvoir? Was she really offered over a hundred and thirty thousand dollars a year to return to Stanford? And will Femineutics prove the fulfillment of her lifelong ambition -- the founding of a department in which she would constitute the sole faculty member and occupy a chair in her own name? You are yanked back from your reflections by her shrill voice; she is ranting now.

"And let me tell you something! That little bitch will never be a team player. What right has she to become a part of this or any other institution? How can you take someone with a name like 'Lola' at all seriously? I'm positive she's sleeping with that odious offense to Femalehood, Herbert Blake. Not that she could ever mean a thing to him! Well, aren't you going to agree with me?"

When you manage to vocalize, apologetically, that you are not a member of the tenure committee, that, in fact, you are a French teacher from the local academy, or a visiting lecturer from a small college in the South, she seems suddenly to deflate. Her eyes return to their sockets, the crimson dissipates on her cheeks. She is almost smiling again when she slips her long, surprisingly firm, free arm into one of yours and directs you toward the refreshment table.

"Oh, then may I offer you some cake?"

Ad aspera ad astra

Through adversity to the stars

Harold Lang

Associate Professor with Tenure

Department of Biochemistry

Salary: $46,000

Sometimes the best thing that can happen to a person is when the person fails at the thing that means the most.

Professor Lang packed up his satchel and prepared to leave the lecture hall. He never ceased to be amazed when, as was invariably the case, a crowd of students gathered to wait for him at the door. They would have questions about the lecture, or they would just be nervous about the upcoming exam, or they needed letters of recommendation. One would want nothing more than to confide in him that his sister was getting married next week, another to tell him about the death of a grandparent, still another to express concerns about her career choices. God, thought Harold, I'm the last person to help them with their personal problems. But he would have the time for each of them. That, according to one of his few friends in the Biochemistry Department, was his mistake. But how could that be a mistake? Harold had spent the past twenty-five years trying to figure this out.

Harold Lang was old before his time. In fact, Harold could not recall if he had ever had a time. Success had raced past him without so much as a smile of recognition. He was unsure even now exactly when things had changed, and the reasons for which he had been hired by the university became the reasons for which he was ignored and ostracized by those who had come long after him.

Professor Lang was that rarest of all beings on the modern university campus: a teacher. That is to say, teaching was his primary responsibility to himself, as well as to the university. And he was effective and successful in this vocation. His students, past and present, admired and respected him and inevitably went on to accomplish great things in the field. To reward Harold for his unusual talents, his department gave him numerous commendations and recognition. And they slowly took away his laboratory space. And they never promoted him to Full Professor, he was always Associate Professor with tenure, trapped in a deep chasm somewhere between the junior faculty and the senior faculty.

When he had finally extricated himself from the mob, he walked back the rest of the way to his office, brooding -- but even in this he was unsuccessful, he could not maintain the cynicism of his colleagues, he lacked their bitterness and their sophistication. Max Stern, for example, was a man who had been kind to him in the beginning and was now barely civil to him. Max, to Harold's way of thinking, had no right to either the power or the prestige that came with his title. Alvin Boyd was nothing but a used-car salesman in a lab coat. Fanny, after an unsuccessful play for his affections, now simply rode all over him. And Lucretia Vasquez-Lopez -- she was too horrible to consider.

Once in his office -- incidentally the smallest excuse for an office that his department dared to pass off as a tenured faculty member's workplace, occupying less space than the Xeroxing room and having no window -- Harold was delighted at the rare message that the secretary had left him. He was to call Professor Boyd. It had been over a year since he had last spoken to his chairman, a man elusive even among his friends, much less with so embarrassing an associate as Harold. When he dialed the extension, the chairman's secretary responded.

"Yes, this is Professor Lang. I have a message here to get in touch with Professor Boyd." And he savored his final phrase, "The message says it's urgent."

"Oh, yes, Mr. Lang," said the woman, who projected a superior tone more appropriate to the wife of the President of the University than to Alvin Boyd's latest in a rapidly changing series of secretaries. "Professor Boyd asked me to tell you that it wouldn't be necessary for you to meet with the candidate for the new faculty position this afternoon."

But Professor Lang was genuinely interested in meeting with prospective faculty. "Oh, I don't mind at all. I was quite looking forward to it."

The secretary gave a little chuckle. "I'm afraid you don't understand, Professor Lang. Chairman Boyd would rather you not meet with the applicant. It's very important that the young man have an opportunity to talk to several other faculty members, and he probably won't have time for you."

Professor Lang was dismayed. "But I wouldn't need a lot of time --"

The secretary interrupted him with a sigh, louder and more peremptory than Harold's normal tone of voice. Then she brought the conversation to a close. "Listen, Lang, Boyd says you're not, under any circumstances, to come anywhere near new or prospective faculty members." The click of the receiver slamming down was like a gunshot for Harold, but he had been taking this sort of shellfire for years.

In fact, moments later he had filed this latest humiliation away under Professional Sorrows, in a mental folder that was already enormous and still growing; he would no doubt remember it in bed tonight. Meanwhile, he threw himself into writing the letter of reference for a graduating senior who had always done excellent work in Harold's classes. The terrible fear crept up on him once again that a letter from him meant almost nothing outside of the university, because he himself had never fulfilled his own scholastic promise. Was it, then, cowardice which prevented him from publishing ten articles a year and chairing six committees and gossiping about the untenured women and using them as he pleased? Might he not have been both a good teacher and a respected scholar? He tried to think of someone who could claim to have achieved this double feat, but there was no one. The Great Paradox remained; an interest in your students and a desire to share your knowledge with them inevitably proved disastrous to academic aspirations. If you could talk to your students -- and what is worse, if you were _seen_ to talk to them -- then it was assumed that you had no time for anything else, and that, intellectually speaking, you were probably at or below their level. And Harold would never give up his students.

So he began the letter, a soliloquy on his own inadequacy to comment upon so brilliant a pupil as David Rice. And it was all true and it would arrive before the due date and those who received it would smile and think, "What faculty member ever had time to turn in a letter of recommendation early?" For Harold, however cruelly, or at best patronizingly, people may have treated him, had a profound and uncanny understanding of his own implausibility.

After spending the next three hours preparing his undergraduate lecture, he once again, and this time somewhat wearily, packed his papers into his satchel and prepared to leave. There was the usual conflict. Should he take this grant application home and work on it? But then he remembered that his granddaughter was visiting and his wife was making a special meal for them. Afterward, they had promised to take her to the park. And then perhaps they would drive along the water. They might even stop to look for shells, if the sun hadn't set.

Vas deferens

Hans Reuther

Full Professor,

Department of Biophysics

Salary: $75,000

Hans Reuther surveyed the young female standing in front of him. Nice legs, good ass, slender waist, chest maybe a little smaller than he usually liked. Still, she was worth noticing, if for no other reason than that she was there and she had female characteristics. Hans rather liked the surprise visits of the undergraduate girls from his courses, as a matter of fact it was arguable that they represented the only pleasure he took in teaching. He pulled out a chair so that the girl could sit down.

She was saying something about the course. Hans tried in vain to drag his mind from tallying up her physical pros and cons.

"Yes, yes," he said, drawing himself up behind his desk and inflating his chest. Now they both had a better view.

She was dressed in the usual undergraduate garb, jeans that were slightly baggy and a loose sweatshirt. Perhaps underneath it all she wasn't as small as he thought. Suddenly, when she raised her hand to emphasize a point, a tiny crimson triangle of the girl's bra strap winked at him from inside the collar of her shirt. Typical, he thought, for these girls to dress like football players in training on the outside and expensive escorts underneath. He felt as though someone had struck a match and brought it close to his loins.

"Of course, of course," he said, anxious to provide no obstacle to the train of her thoughts or the flow of her words, which continued to wash over him like a stream in which he saw, along with his own, the reflection of his Echo.

He thought he felt her foot under the desk. It may have been the leg of her chair. He tensed and quivered inwardly. She was rather animated now, or at least he thought she must be, given the quick rising and falling of her -- as it turned out, quite ample -- chest. He stood up, ostensibly to stretch, but actually to get a better look at her from behind. When she seemed to have paused, he hastened to fill the gap.

"I understand completely."

What was she talking about? he wondered. It didn't matter. The line of her neck and shoulders reminded him of the smooth curves of the red blood cells he had recently viewed under his high-powered microscope. Or was it vice versa, and the graceful silhouettes of the cells had led him to dream of the contours before him now?

Suddenly, and to his horror, she stood up. She was leaving. She handed him a form, which momentarily blocked his view of her hips. At this moment he would have signed anything. When she leaned over to retrieve it, talking all the time, he smelled her soap and shared with her the shower she had clearly just taken. He stood up again and rested his hand on her shoulder as she moved toward the door. Under the pretext of holding it open for her, he in fact prevented the girl from gaining access to the hallway, thereby prolonging his exposure to the undergraduate point of view. Finally, taking a deep breath which Hans felt in his own diaphragm, the girl managed to squeeze through the narrow opening he had begrudgingly allowed.

Without the girl to distract him, Professor Reuther was forced to return to his work. He went first to collect his film from the electron microscope. The latter was a gargantuan, columnar instrument. He performed the ritual of opening it with unconscious grace and care, stroking the correct buttons and easing the door to gain entry. He always felt most at home in the dark, seeing with his hands, every dial and knob, every surface and joint, which parts rotated, which went up and down, which remained fixed. He gingerly removed the film canister and carried it deeper into the dark confines of his *sanctum sanctorum*.

There, beneath the red light, Hans spread out his negatives and prepared the baths. After developing and rinsing, he hung his wet treasures to dry. Then came his favorite part, the selection process. Choosing which micrographs to publish in his next article was relatively easy; a more difficult task was ranking the numerous images of young women he had collected over the past week.

Here they were, like so many contestants at an international beauty pageant. Many of them had agreed to be photographed and had even posed for Hans in a variety of suggestive attitudes. Others he had sighted on campus through the large, foreign telephoto lens of which he was so proud. Now all of them paraded before him, challenging or provoking or demurely acquiescing. It was for this that his scientist father had fled Nazi Germany.

The room smelled of perspiration and developing fluid. He remembered that he hadn't told that girl about his extra office hours next week. The prints dripped into the pans. He hardly remembered what the girl looked like. In the red light, he watched his shadow lengthening.

When he returned to his office, he was dismayed to find no one waiting for him. He walked in and sat down, in order to file the micrographs in a drawer of his desk. When the phone rang, his spiral fall back to reality was complete; it was his wife. She wanted to know if he could stop and pick up the boys at school. And should she make soup for dinner? Or would they go out?

Amor vincit omnia

Love conquers all

Rachel Glum

Associate Professor with Tenure,

Department of English Literature

Salary: $51,500

It was ridiculous, all this Catholic guilt -- for God's sake, she was Jewish! And Herbert was at best a lapsed high church Episcopalian. So where did they come from, her recurring visions of Christ and the Woman Taken in Adultery? She was haunted -- by Herbert, by guilt, by increasingly slim hopes for marriage.

And where was he anyway? Rachel threw the book she wasn't reading across the bed. It was bound to be boring. Who could take seriously an anthology of critical essays on earlier criticisms of the original reviews of Joyce's *Finnegan's Wake*? Did Herbert really read this stuff? And if so, why couldn't he just summarize it for her?

Rachel thought proudly of her own book, *The Hardest Times: Unmarried Mothers and Widows and Social Dynamics in Dickens's Early Stories and Novels, with Commentary on his Correspondence.* It had come out almost three years ago, and she had yet to read the final version, after Herbert's thorough rewriting and editing. But in this, at least, she trusted him.

How did she ever get into this mess? A simple recital of the facts reduced her to laughter and tears. She had been hired fresh out of graduate school, a timid twenty-eight-year-old, every bit as naive as when she had first left home for a prestigious, all girl, East-Coast college. In the subsequent decade of expensive education among the most celebrated and sophisticated teachers, she had learned nothing of life. When she took this job, she already had the sensation that, as a woman, she was beginning to rot on the bough. Consequently, older male members of the faculty, for whom her dominant father had in any case provided her with a predisposition, found her ripe for the picking, were in fact delighted at the way she dropped into their waiting hands.

But of course she had made a few mistakes early on. Her first three affairs were with untenured professors like herself, a clear proof of her ignorance which nevertheless enhanced her desirability among her older suitors. She moved rapidly from these flings to an equal number of far more problematic liaisons with tenured, and in some cases famous, faculty, two of whom were, to all intents and purposes, senile; the third, Max Stern, was the only one who survived the relationship. Finally she had been passed by Max to Herbert Blake, who proved the ideal companion. He was in her own department, and so could be used to further her career. He was, like most of the others, married, so there was no need for a commitment which might arrest her movement up the ladder. And the oddest thing of all, she liked him, and came to depend on him as a friend. So comfortable had this relationship become, in fact, that it was now in its ninth year, during the last six of which she had been surprised to hear him talking about marriage, and even more surprised to find herself listening.

Now, on the down side of the sine curve of her romance, the references to a possible future together were dwindling, and Rachel found herself rather desperately clinging to a man whom she had originally viewed as merely a convenient stepping stone. It was true that, in the academic sense, he had been faithful, waging a fierce campaign to win her tenure. And they had been up against some serious competition. Henry Clawson Binker, then chairman of the English Department, had, unluckily for Rachel, taken up with another untenured and extensively available junior professor by the name of Claudia Holt, at about the same time Rachel had been tagged by Herbert. Even if they had not been pitted against one other in the academic arena, even if they had been perfect strangers from different professional spheres, Claudia and Rachel would eventually have come to blows, over a dress or cosmetic counter or on their knees, wrestling for the same pair of shoes. They were very much alike: pretty, pretty nervous, pretty selfish, extremely ambitious.

And Rachel had won. She rolled over on the bed, still light-hearted reliving her victory of five years before. Ms. Holt's appointment had not been renewed by the department, nor by Chairman Binker, who slunk back, as he did every two or three years, to his moneyed wife, a signal to the latter that it was her own turn to go fishing in the untenured faculty pool. And Rachel, all of a sudden, found herself with everything she had always wanted, a permanent position at one of the greatest universities in the country, a published work recognized for its insight and grammatical originality, and an intelligent man in the prime of his life.

And where was he now?

Rachel studied the clockface by her bed, as if to stare it down, to force from it an admission of inaccuracy. It could not be half past four already. When you had only the weekday afternoons, little things like an hour delay mattered, especially on Monday.

Why couldn't Herbert just leave his wife?, she asked herself for the thousandth time. But she knew it would never be that easy. If the Binkers wanted to alternate in their adulterous adventures, that was fine, in fact it confirmed that they were well-matched, sharing, if nothing else, the same moral turpitude. Herbert, on the other hand, had, morally speaking, married up; his wife, whom Rachel had seen only once from the back seat of a car, was something of a paragon in academic circles. Every bit as intelligent as her husband, as well-spoken, as educated, as attractive -- in short, his female equivalent in everything but his faults of character -- Maggie Blake remained to this day an aspect of her husband's ambitions, the last vestige of his youthful ideals. For this reason, as Rachel was coming to realize, Herbert would never let her go. He might sleep with Rachel every afternoon, Monday through Friday, and take long, ostensibly scholastic, trips with her, but every night he returned to Maggie and the memories, sometimes frustrating and seemingly unbearable but constant and unaccusing, of a time when he was worthy of her.

But how was it that Rachel -- the other woman, the Woman Taken in Adultery -- knew all of this? How had she come to understand things of which Herbert himself seemed oblivious? How had she grown to sympathize with this woman whom at the same time she hated with a fervor that made her feelings for Claudia Holt seem mild and tame by comparison? And of course the energy she spent tangling and untangling her web with Herbert was no longer available for developing her own scholastic interests and fulfilling the early promise she had shown. Even her teaching, for which she had once been popular, had fallen off; her dedication to her students was ridiculed by Herbert, for whom pedagogy had never represented a serious component of the academic commitment. But she had loved teaching, long before she had loved him.

When she thought about these things she grew morose, she didn't want him near her, she wanted, like all the Fallen, to be alone.

And then at last, thank God!, the doorbell rang.

Equo ne credite, Teucri!

Do not trust the horse, Trojans

Margaret Fanshaw

Full Professor,

Department of Cellular Biology

Salary: $101,000

T he only noise to be heard in the enormous conference room was the sneeze of a shy graduate student, followed by the sound of him blowing his nose.

"Save that!"

The voice of Professor Margaret "Fanny" Fanshaw cracked like a whip. It was her only joke, and she repeated it at least four times a day.

The room resounded with polite laughter. For Professor Fanshaw, this sneeze meant business, its byproducts were the object of all her scientific attention, in a way her *raison d'être*. Fanny had garnered for the University a staggering fortune in federal and private grant monies in order to support her research on mucous membranes and their secretional activity. She left no gland unturned in her quest for the true nature of mucal tissue. She had made enormous strides in the field which was, it must be acknowledged, almost exclusively her own.

Today was the biweekly meeting of Margaret Fanshaw's laboratory, which had the largest staff of any department in any of the scientific fields at this university. As on a well-run farm, there was an enormous number of hands -- post-doctoral fellows, graduate students, undergraduate interns, technicians and even a few unidentifiable hangers-on -- all of them in a constant struggle to be closest to Fanny, to stroke her, to pat her, to pop sugar cubes into her mouth. For they all depended on Fanny, a fact of which she was happy to remind them at every opportunity.

Fanny cantered into the room and placed her hind quarters daintily on the seat always left empty for her at the head of the table. She recognized the presence of each member of her laboratory with a slow nod of her head in his or her direction, a ritual which took no little time and energy, as Fanny's staff numbered well over thirty. When she had finished her first slurp of steaming coffee and had taken the first drag on her extra slim, filtered cigarette, exhaling the smoke through her nose, she brought the meeting to order by clearing her throat loudly.

"Well, the first thing I want to bring up today concerns the time commitment that you have all made to this lab and to me, though some of you seem to have forgotten it. Perhaps we'd better review my rules and expectations. To begin with, I will not tolerate tardiness. If I can be ready to work at six o'clock every morning, so can all of you!"

It was true. Fanny was always out of the stable and at the starting gate by sunup.

"Perhaps some of you aren't as eager to get to your work as you ought to be. Well, I can promise you that there are substitutes waiting for any one of you who feels less enthusiastic than when I first honored you by taking you into this lab."

There was absolute silence among her staff at this unfeeling reminder of their replaceability. Only a fly, buzzing loudly about Fanny's head, dared to question her authority. With one flick of her thick hand, she batted it to the ground, where it lay dazed for the remainder of the meeting.

"Furthermore, no graduate student of mine should ever want or need to return home before ten o'clock at night. If you have time for socializing, you have time to be working on your mucal cultures. Needless to say, post-doctoral fellows should show even greater dedication. When I was a girl, I lived in my advisor's lab."

This, however, was not altogether true. She had lived in her advisor's house, during the long vacations his wife had taken. Nor is it entirely certain that Fanny was ever a girl, for even when she was young her features were more those of a foal than of an adolescent human female. Unfortunately for Fanny, this resemblance to the horse became increasingly apparent as she grew older. Now, at forty-five, she was a fully developed nag.

Fanny ran her tongue over her prominent teeth, a gesture which in no way prepared her audience for the vitriol of her subsequent climactic demand. "What do you all take me for!?" she brayed.

No one raised their hand. Fanny had them right where she wanted them, cowering and afraid, each one praying that it might be his or her neighbor who got bitten or kicked. For they knew that the moment had arrived for their leader to become brutally selective and personal.

"Miss Pingree," she began after a long, nasal sigh. "I don't care if your father did build a wing of the library, if you can't take shorter lunches you should try not eating at all."

Though Fanny herself was not a large woman, her small frame only emphasized the enormity of her head.

"And, Mr. Salter, did you honestly believe that I would allow you to attend the departmental retreat, much less give a presentation on a Monday afternoon? I have withdrawn your name from the list of attendees."

One after another, beginning with Miss Pingree and Mr. Salter, Fanny chewed up the workers she had chosen to chastise. After treating nine or ten of them in this manner, she seemed to grow drowsy and indifferent, and her head began to droop. It took the contradiction of one of her undergraduate interns to rouse her from her monotonous bleating.

"I beg your pardon?! Are you saying that you will be returning to Japan for over a week in the middle of the term?" Fanny physically reared up before the possibility of mutiny among her dependents.

"Well, it is Thanksgiving weekend. And I didn't go home at all last summer." The young woman, Sook Yee, was not to be deterred.

After a moment, Fanny recovered her equanimity. She remembered that within two weeks another Asian would be entering her lab. And this one would be the real thing, People's Republic, desperately poor, and servile. Then Fanny could let Sook Yee go.

But she wouldn't say anything just now. She would wait till the new girl arrived. That would be less risky. No one could accuse Fanny of not having horse sense.

Non sum qualis eram

I am not what I once was

Herbert Blake

Full Professor,

Department of English Literature

Salary: $77,500

After seven -- or was it nine? -- years, it was time to nip this thing in the bud.

Herbert Blake left his office more reluctantly every day. A little later every afternoon. And this growing tendency was in no way due to a revived interest in his scholastic pursuits. Nor was it the indication of a newfound zeal in the preparation of his courses, nor of a sudden sentimental interest in the academic welfares of his students. The reason for this gradual shift in his daily routine could only be ascribed to a decline in the organization of his personal affairs, and to an increasing awareness of their absurdity.

Herbert made his way slowly down the stairs of Maxwell Hall, like a man recovering from surgery on both knees. And he couldn't help but recall, every day at this stage in his funereal progress across campus, that once he had been positively spry, and full of physical and intellectual vigor. How had he gotten himself into this mess?

He thought without emotion -- with the cold objectivity for which his literary criticism had once been acclaimed -- of his early days at the university. He had been innocent, had shone like a choirboy among the shadier gangster types of the English department. Conscientious to a fault, and loyal to all the academic ideals, he had been the boast of the administration for his perfect balance of scholarly activity and pedagogical service. In fact, he was one of the most popular teachers in the history of the school. But that had all changed when he received tenure. When his position had been secured, he stopped performing for his former judges. His scholastic endeavors became more and more personal and introspective, as though, in his books on Spenser and Milton, he was speaking not to contemporary readers but in a private language to the dust about whom he wrote. And to all intents and purposes, his teaching ended the day he signed his permanent contract. By now he could no longer tolerate good teaching among his peers.

And his personal life had followed the same basic trajectory. He had married, at twenty five, a beautiful and intelligent Bostonian like himself. They had their first child to celebrate his first promotion, and twins when his tenure seemed assured. He considered himself, even now, a family man. Once only, quite early on, he had made the required attempt to have an extramarital affair with an older, tenured faculty member, Hannah Dartmouth. At the recollection, his eyes reflexively squeezed shut in order to contain the shudder which shook his entire nervous system. She had accepted him, to his horror, and then, at the crucial moment, he had fled back to his wife and family. He was intended by nature to be a faithful man, but at some point, and in spite of all he had learned from his near miss with Hannah, his needle had skipped its groove, and he had wakened up with another woman, feeling suddenly that he must be faithful to her, too.

And at this moment, three streets away, in the spacious apartment which Herbert had found and initially helped to finance, she was waiting for him, this other woman, filing her nails or pretending to read. Not that she was stupid, in fact she had been a very promising addition to the department at a time when women scholars were at a premium and still quite rare. Nonetheless, Herbert would never have noticed her had not Max Stern, in one of their very infrequent bar visits together, raved about her incessantly, so that when Herbert finally expressed his awe, more facetiously than seriously, Max popped her into his colleague's mouth like a cocktail olive.

At first the arrangement had seemed like a dream. She wasn't the least bit interested in commitment and was more content even than Herbert to meet only on weekday afternoons. This apparent independence had come to preoccupy her lover, making him suspicious and jealous and, consequently, like a new husband; it was natural to talk to her of leaving his wife and starting over, because neither of them believed it could ever happen. That was after all what they shared: a love of fiction.

But with the passing years, Herbert came increasingly to feel that in the mathematical division of his time between two females and their worlds, his spirit was also halved, and suffering. What is more, the older he got, the more obvious it became that he had less and less to share with either woman. He was haunted and embarrassed by the recurring image of both of his partners trying desperately to make a full meal from the leftovers of yesterday's feast. He was sick at heart, in the truest sense, because he was sick of himself.

But, he could not deny, however ungenerous he might seem, that he was also sick of this other woman. Sick of her constant jabbering, her demands, her threats to appear at his home at dinner time, dressed in rags and ringing a bell. And he was sick, too, of the unchanging inscrutability of his wife, which forced him to flee to the other, while keeping him tethered to the idea of something permanent which she personified. In short, he was a man with two distinct diseases, each of which offered some relief from the other, but either of which must inevitably prove fatal.

Had there never been a day, he asked himself, approaching the woman's apartment, had there never been a moment when he had felt truly happy? No, since his first reading of _King Lear_ at the age of seventeen, everything had gone downhill.

Instead of sounding the buzzer of his second home, he decided to walk around the block once more. Yesterday he had circled the place three times; today, he thought, perhaps four. But it was a whirlpool, and he would eventually be dragged down.

Veni, vidi, vici

I came, I saw, I conquered

Derek Renaud

Assistant Professor,

Department of Cellular Biology

Salary: $54,000

It remains to be seen to what extent we determine our facial features -- not our expressions, but the actual shapes and sizes of the components of that human billboard, the head. In Derek Renaud's case, there could be no question. He had worked hard and long to give to his jaw its perfect point, the jut that represented a noticeable advance on his father's similar but comparatively homebound silhouette. So, too, with the son's nose, which had been trained like an orchid, upward and outward, flowering grandly in the exact center of his face. And one eyebrow, it goes without saying, was permanently cocked.

Derek was young, although he appeared to be younger than he was, due no doubt to a concentrated effort to appear as effortlessly boyish as possible, without actually wearing a baseball cap or riding a skateboard. He had the expression of someone who never ceases to be startled by his own extraordinary energy. He skipped, rather than walked, down the hall to the Xerox machine. In actuality, he was beside himself with anger because he had no secretary who could be burdened with performing these idiotic tasks. In fact, the chairman, Alvin Boyd, had circulated a memo specifically condemning junior faculty use of departmental secretaries for photocopying, a decision which had led Derek to applaud his chairman's wisdom in the public forum of a recent faculty meeting.

Derek peeked his head into the room with the photocopier, a monstrous machine which left very little space for the user. Of course, there was already somebody using it, but Derek was incensed to recognize this somebody as a graduate student, and a female graduate student at that.

"I hope you're finishing soon," Derek demanded in a tone which suggested that he would accept only an affirmative response.

The graduate student in question, Elizabeth Hopkins, looking slightly disconcerted, stammered a brief explanation of her situation. "Well, I do have the machine all set up for collating copies of my dissertation. My advisor wanted -- "

But Derek did not wait for the whole story. Like others of his species he was pressed for time. He merely raised his chin, as though expecting the student to duck out of the way of the death blow it might deliver. When Elizabeth did not move, Derek adopted more drastic measures.

"Well that's very easy to fix," he smiled, as he bent down and unplugged the machine. "You know very well that graduate students have no priority when it comes to the use of this machine. Some of us here have far more important business than Xeroxing our entire theses."

Flashing defiance, Elizabeth gathered up her papers and hastily exited the room. Derek forgot about her the moment she was gone. He busily began setting up the machine for his own copying, of a memo which had no other purpose than to prove that it had been written. The first copy, he noted with some disgust, came out on heavy, dissertation-bond paper, forcing him to open up the machine, and though he briefly considered continuing to copy on this material, he was afraid it might appear pretentious to other faculty. In the midst of trying to unjam the second copy, Professor Fanshaw strode in.

"I hope you haven't broken the machine," she cackled brusquely. "I need something copied *toute de suite.*"

Derek paused momentarily, then smiled deferentially. "Of course, Fanny, let me just fix everything for you. Some stupid graduate student screwed up the machine." Derek knew before he had spoken that Professor Fanshaw could be counted on to have a dread of graduate students equal to his own.

Fanny tapped her foot loudly, snorting at the delay. "Well anyway, it's good to see you busy," she whinnied, after a pause.

When Derek extricated himself from his awkward position half inside the machine, Fanny flopped down her huge load.

"Well, don't just stand there, start feeding them in," she commanded.

Derek did not allow his agitation to show. In fact he beamed like the loving son Fanny would never have. After all, it wasn't worth risking a tenure vote for a few extra minutes at the photocopier. With a great show of vim, Derek divided his attention between Fanny's self-absorbed monologue about her innumerable research projects and Xeroxing what seemed an infinite number of her laboratory's financial reports. When he finally finished, nearly an hour later, he hand delivered the resulting pile to Professor Fanshaw, who was by this time taking her last sip of coffee in the faculty lounge next door.

Upon returning to the photocopier, he was taken aback to discover yet another colleague in possession. But this one, Dr. Shrimpton, was at the same untenured level in the hierarchy as Derek himself. The two rivals confronted one another, their mutual antagonism barely hidden behind masks of indifference and imperturbable superiority.

"Excuse me, but I was using that machine," Derek announced, his nose at its zenith.

Dr. Shrimpton looked as though Derek had addressed him in a primitive and incomprehensible tongue, and continued to use the copier. Derek considered unplugging the machine again, but then reconsidered; it was best to use subtlety when teaching intellectual inferiors a lesson. He was about to tell Shrimpton to go and fuck himself, when the departmental secretary, Mrs. Broadloom, attempted to squeeze her person into the room.

"Pardon me, dears," she chimed, "I hate to interrupt, but there's a reporter on the phone who says he's from _Laboratory Life_ and he wants to talk to Dr. Shrimpton. Something about a photo spread on his latest project."

Shrimpton seemed to have wakened from the trance induced by the monotonous hum of the photocopier. Still without acknowledging the presence of his colleague, but with a great demonstration of condescension, he took Mrs. Broadloom by the hand and helped to squeeze her back out the door, all the time telling her that this was the third magazine that had contacted him today and that at this rate he would have to hold a press conference.

Angrier than ever, Derek bent down to begin what should have been a ten-minute task. It was a small consolation that Shrimpton had forgotten to remove half of his papers; these Derek promptly dropped into the waste basket. Another secretary opened the door, but upon seeing Derek's expression quickly retreated. Derek's copying was finally getting under way when the door opened yet again to reveal the face of Elizabeth Hopkins, as though returned from the dead.

"If graduate students spent half the time writing their dissertations that they do blocking the machines to copy them, this department might produce some worthwhile scientists. I would suggest that you go home and do your laundry -- maybe you'll have better luck with the dormitory washers and dryers."

But the door had not yet closed. Accompanying Elizabeth was her advisor, Max Stern, whom she had just happened to meet near the rear entrance of the building. Upon hearing that she had not been able to complete the copying of her dissertation, Professor Stern had seemed uncharacteristically interested in her problems and happily returned with her to the machine to insure that 1) she would be able to furnish him with the text of her thesis immediately, and 2) he would not risk unwanted confrontations with discontent and barely coherent employees upstairs in his lab.

If in fact Dr. Stern actually heard Derek's sarcastic admonitions to Elizabeth, it did not show in his face. Derek, on the other hand, was violently shaken, the barometers of his nose and chin dropping dramatically. Max spoke.

"I am sure you understand that I require a copy of my student's dissertation urgently. I assume there will be no more power failures which might interrupt her work FOR ME."

Derek bobbed, like a bird on a perch, all features drawn inward now. Elizabeth, bending to put the dissertation-bond paper back into the machine, might have been pecking for newly scattered seeds. Only Max, peering down from the heights, remained unruffled.

Procul o procul este, profani

Far off oh keep far off

Interlude: Faculty Wives

T he Triangle Room, located on the *piano nobile* of the Polygon Club, was the most elegant and exclusive meeting place on campus. According to the rules, only faculty members, their families and guests, could be put up and fed at the Polygon, a sort of provincial, academic version of the Pierre or Brown's Hotel. On the second Tuesday of every month, the "Tri" was reserved for the regular luncheon of the only club more exclusive than the "Poly" itself, that of the Faculty Wives.

Mrs. Feldman, always the first to arrive, was shocked and angered to discover that although it was Autumn outside, the interior of the Triangle Room -- *her* Triangle Room (for no one had eaten more meals between these three distressed pecan walls, no one had flirted with more Nobel Prize-winning scientists and Pulitzer Prize-winning playwrights, albeit with little success, than Gloria Feldman) -- still bore all the floral trappings of mid summer. She had so looked forward to the traditional cornucopia and the dried leaf arrangements on the little mahogany tables that filled the room, like a *corps de ballet* in formation, each with its white linen tablecloth laden with crystal and china and silver shooting a pattern of glittering reflections upon the high, medallioned white stucco ceiling.

A shrill greeting brought an abrupt end to Gloria's negative assessment of the room, or rather, redirected her critical gaze. It was Gloria's very best friend, the second Mrs. Everett Morris.[1] As they

---

[1]The reader will recall that there are in fact three Mrs. Morrisses. The first recently moved

embraced, each woman was genuinely pleased to see her companion somewhat dowdily decked out in unflattering colors and cuts. It was this spirit of communal feeling which prevailed among the faculty wives and made them more than a club, made them, in fact, one great female animal with a hundred and forty legs.

In the foyer, Mrs. Reuther paused to check her hairdo in the Chippendale mirror. Behind her, her best friend, Lucy Buchman, waited her turn. Though still young, Mrs. Reuther was no longer in possession of the splendid figure her husband had married. In her overly tight yellow skirt, she was now endowed with something more than the usual pair of buttocks, a criss-cross of straps dividing her posterior into at least seven distinct lobes. Lucy Buchman pretended not to notice, but secretly thanked God that she had managed to avoid a comparable fate, blaming her friend's misfortune on an eating disorder resulting from Professor Reuther's well-known perversities and lack of familial commitment.

When both ladies had finished preening and primping and smoothing and fluffing, they, too, entered the room, which was now filling fast. Most of the members had known each other for years, so the conversational tone was light and familiar, its pitch high if not positively shrill. Those few newcomers, such as Professor Renaud's young wife, the former Miss Marisa Buttrey, were warmly welcomed, fussed over like orphaned calves by competing mother cows whose own offspring had long since been carted away. There was one awkward moment following the arrival of Libby Swallow, wife of this year's Distinguished Poet-in-Residence. As predicted, given her great wealth and privileged background, the sixty-three year old Mrs. Swallow appeared at her first meeting of the Faculty Wives looking perfectly lovely; her hair was dyed the same exquisite teal as her Mercedes, a note intensified in the deeper blue of her handbag and shoes; her jewelry, from the diamond bracelet to a large emerald on her lapel, was impeccable (though Mrs. Hopkins found the emerald paradoxically showy and suspicious); and her Chanel suit, of a silk and wool blend, was quite simply a museum piece. But it was this suit which caused a stir -- and not merely of envy -- among the assembled women, for while Mrs. Swallow was wearing the jacket, she had

---

away from the University. Her absence is much
deplored by both the second and third Mrs.
Morrisses. The third, which is to say present,
Mrs. Morris is said to prefer both of her
predecessors to her husband, but this may be a
rare instance of academic scandal-mongering.

apparently forgotten the skirt, entering the club in the unmistakable lace-edged and shiny fabric of her slip. General relief was felt when, moments later, Mrs. Swallow's chauffeur arrived bearing the bottom half of her ensemble, and laying it discreetly in her lap. Libby only smiled merrily, her sapphire eyes sparkling, and muttered something apologetic about how anxious she had been to arrive on time.

The excitement over Mrs. Swallow's skirt having died down, new conversational clatches formed, grew and dissolved like bubbles in a boiling pot. When the third Mrs. Morris finally freed herself from the spastic caresses of old Mrs. Cuttle, she made a bee-line for her dearest friend, the second Mrs. Morris.

"I've just had a call from Ivy.[2] She's doing FABulously in St. Louis! She's invited us both for a visit."

Further conversation between the two dear chums was interrupted when their nominal chairwoman, Mrs. Alvin Boyd, clapped her hands, and shooed everyone who had not yet done so, to take their seats. Despite the distance between tables, the topics of conversation remained uncannily consistent among all the women, changing only with the appearance of a new course.

With cocktails, for example, was served the latest gossip about poor Maggie Blake's travails. Naturally everybody knew of Mrs. Herbert Blake's sufferings, and everyone present understood her reasons for absenting herself from such gatherings. The destroyer of Maggie's home life, Professor Rachel Glum, was described in terms usually reserved for the Anti-Christ, though it was unclear whether Rachel sinned more grievously in having an affair with a faculty member or in being a faculty member herself.

All the ladies were still engaged in heaping opprobrium on Rachel Glum when the _hors d'oeuvres_ were carried in. These consisted of delicate little pastries filled with crab. Everyone got in their last word on Ms. Glum, and then the conversation shifted ninety degrees to the upcoming annual charity benefit, organized each year by the poor, absent Maggie Blake. Although officially an event sponsored and organized by the Faculty Wife Association (FWA), no one but Mrs. Blake ever volunteered for any of the real work, preferring to wait until the occasion was planned in its entirety before taking up the burden of buying a new dress and actually attending. This year's event was to be a masquerade to benefit the Pediatric Department of the University

---

[2]Ivy Maxwell, the first Mrs. Morris.

Hospital. There was no charity dearer to the communal heart of the Faculty Wives. Each of these women saw in the children's wing a chance for redemption, a second (and, by implication, second-hand) chance at child-rearing, an occupation at which they had almost to a man failed the first time around. And what better prey for the desperate, maternal appetite than a small and helpless bed-ridden one?

After the crab puffs came the chowder, and with the chowder came Mrs. Harold Lang. So great was her aversion to the small talk which preceded every luncheon, that she was regularly appallingly late. In fact, she only came for her husband's sake, thinking that her absence might provide yet another reason for withholding his promotion. To the other faculty wives, her absence meant no more than her presence, as she was entirely lacking in chic and had for years refused to have her house redecorated. Nor had they ever forgiven her for her greatest *faux pas*, her Original Sin, having dared, eighteen years ago, to bring her five-year-old daughter to one of these lunches.

Between the soup and the main course -- a poached salmon steak on a bed of spinach -- there was a general intermission, during which it was the custom to criticize faculty wives who failed to attend these meetings. For the third time, the second Mrs. Morris had to explain to old Mrs. Cuttle that there was no Mrs. Frank Larry. There had been a Mrs. Sertz, but her husband, before divorcing her, had transformed her into an administrator, thereby rendering her unrecognizable as a woman. The relative newcomer, Mrs. Renaud, remarked loudly and often on the absence of the wife of her husband's rival, Mrs. Shrimpton. It was true that Mrs. Shrimpton never came, which was rarely noticed, as her existence was unknown to all but a few. In any case, she would never have fit in with the other wives, violating as she did many of their unspoken rules. For example, she was young, attractive and, impossible to forgive, employed. She had even kept her maiden name. So when Mrs. Renaud referred to a "Mrs. Shrimpton" as a post-doctoral fellow in Dr. Stern's laboratory, most of the faculty wives were surprised to hear that Dr. Shrimpton was married, and one of the ladies, Mrs. Polyp, who was the oldest and most august member of the group, nearly choked on a peanut from the cocktail mix, since she was certain that only last week, her youngest daughter had mentioned going on a date with a Dr. Shrimpton. But no doubt she had misheard the name...

Mrs. Stern was as surprised as most of the others to hear that her husband had employed the elusive and overeducated Mrs. Shrimpton. Such comments always gave her pause to think. For she, too, was a woman of considerable intelligence and worldly knowledge, less the perfect companion for, than the female version of, her distinguished husband. There had been a previous Mrs. Stern, but in contrast to the great amity which joined all three Mrs. Morrisses, the present Mrs. Stern had successfully driven her predecessor out of the FWA fold. While she contemplated this latest information, Mrs. Binker, seated opposite, picked at her filet, proving once again that if you pick long enough, you are sure to put on pounds. Such was the silent observation of the second and ONLY Mrs. Stern, who crossed her pencil thin legs and looked away in disgust.

Following the salmon was a palette-cleaning salad laden with baby prawns and salary comparisons. The noise from one table rose above the general din; a rather animated conversation had broken out between Mrs. Buchman and Mrs. Forrest, Lucy Buchman claiming that her husband's salary as Art Museum Director, including fringe benefits such as paintings and sculptures -- estimated at their fair market value, which was the focus of her own cottage research -- was considerably higher than that of any of the administrators at the school, and certainly more than that of the Dean of Graduate Studies. This conclusion was altogether intolerable to Mrs. Forrest, who was hardly on speaking terms with her husband but who had no intention of letting a picture-framer make more money than he, and a pretentious, drunken picture-framer at that. Order was only precariously restored when Chairwoman Boyd, seizing the opportunity to break off Mrs. Renaud's obsequious whining about her own husband's meager salary, stood up and briskly clapped her hands again.

At last, a selection of desserts was brought in. Most of the women, proud of having eaten what they considered a light lunch, opted to reward themselves for this self-control by choosing the flourless chocolate cake with the *de rigueur* raspberry topping. Now the conversation turned to humorous anecdotes -- most of them sheer inventions -- about the Faculty Wife's greatest enemies, female faculty members and graduate students. Before long, the women were venting their anxiety and dislike of nearly everyone outside their closely-knit circle, and a few who ought technically to have fit in. This was truly the climax of the afternoon, the grand finale of the matinee. The cordial glasses of Chambord and Drambuie only sharpened the spurious stories, complete with lewd asides, for as a rule, faculty wives handle their liquor far better than do their mates.

"Promise not to tell."
"Round heels on that one."
"A peignoir she calls a dress."
"The woman's a horse!"

"But Libby, the joke was on her! It turned out to be a black man!"

"Who does she think she is?"

"That Lopez woman actually thought that since she was both faculty and a wife she could join, but we set her straight!"

"Not easygoing, just easy."

"More breasts than morals."

"Jewish. Period."

"Forty-three, my ass!"

"She'll get it back in alimony."

"Neckline is a misnomer!"

"Don't ask me how I know."

"He's what you call a pillow-biter."

"Who does she think SHE is?"

"That's right, tiled in brown, no doubt to match her teeth!"

"She didn't stop with the face-lift, and even for that they must have needed heavy machinery!"

"Catholic. I'll say no more."

"If he leaves her for that one, he's in for a surprise!"

"He wasn't the first. He won't be the last."

"Who DOES she think she IS?"

Slowly, as the afternoon tipped toward evening, the women rose to go. They invariably left in pairs, as they had come. The two Mrs. Morrisses left arm in arm, discussing their future trip to St. Louis. Mrs. Buchman firmly made no farewell to Mrs. Forrest. Mrs. Cuttle tripped as usual on the stair. When everyone else had gone, Mrs. Feldman, deliberately and possessively bestowing upon these lunches a sense of closure, stood up and expressed to the waiting staff her long-simmering dismay at the unseasonable decorations. Then she looked at her watch. It was almost six o'clock. She was due back at the Poly for dinner at eight. She headed toward the bar. "After all," she spoke aloud, though there was nobody nearby, "to go all the way home and then turn around and come back would be utterly pointless."

Caveat emptor

Let the buyer beware

Eunice Lattrey

Assistant Professor,

Department of Art History

Salary: $34,000

Eunice Lattrey sucked long and hard on her cigarette; she could take in more smoke on one drag than any man she knew. It was only the tip of the iceberg of her talent. At last, impatiently, she threw her head back, providing invisible admirers with a perfect view of her extraordinary profile, and exhaled the inordinate quantity of gray vapor which encircled her head like fog about a beacon. Eunice, too, was both bright and pointed. She tapped her foot loudly under her desk, and swung round dramatically when the person on the other end of the line finally responded.

"Yes, this is Professor Lattrey. Eunice Lattrey. I'm calling about my book." Eunice spoke briskly and with a staccato rhythm. She was efficient, indefatigable, always perfunctory and direct.

The voice on the telephone told Eunice that the publishers had not yet received her final payment for the costs of printing her work, entitled, "Dung Art: From Necochea to New York". Getting this book published was proving extremely expensive, Eunice thought, and dealing with the publisher felt more and more like listening to kidnappers whose ransom demands continued to soar. But Eunice never questioned the necessity of the arrangement. She knew that to get tenure nowadays it was essential to show publications -- not just articles, but publications of substance and breadth. Her book, well over one hundred pages, certainly fit that bill.

And the subject of her research was another coup. Eunice glanced at the photograph on her desk, depicting herself, a tall, large-boned white woman surrounded by what looked to be a dozen stark naked, dark-skinned dwarves, each holding an object made of human or animal dung. Eunice couldn't remember if the picture had been taken in Necochea or New York, but it was, without question, a remarkable image. She would send it along with the check; they could use it for the back cover of her book, just below the paragraph describing her as the only white woman who had delved so deeply into primitive cultures, and come back with such an unparalleled artistic trove.

"I'll send it today," Eunice barked, and hung up the phone, recalling once again her good fortune at having stumbled upon this unstaked intellectual territory while on a South American vacation two years ago. Though she officially belonged to the Department of Art History, Eunice the Scholar was impossible to pigeonhole; her work broke all boundaries. This was her greatest strength in the academic community. She was also a shrewd businesswoman, having purchased, for an absurd sum, many of the artifacts she had illustrated and interpreted in her book. This might even lead to a major exhibition, at the Guggenheim or the Museum of Modern Art. She made a note to contact someone with contacts.

Eunice returned to her daily agenda. According to this, in an hour and a half she was scheduled to teach her course on *Shopping as Art*. A quick glance at the syllabus told her that she had promised her pupils a lecture on "Phallic Fingerfoods and Vaginal Snacks." Aside from noting that the final syllable of the word 'phallic' was a homonym for a primary function of the tongue, she had nothing to say. Nor was she able, preoccupied as she naturally was with her book, to remember what she had been thinking of when she made the syllabus. Worst of all, she herself had not yet read the readings she had apparently assigned for this lecture. These facts might have led to panic, or at least created a dilemma, for a less sturdy individual, but Eunice was unflappable. She rifled through textbooks and magazines, articles she had published and those -- far fewer in number -- that she had read, for material that she could transplant into her upcoming class.

Suddenly, in the last issue of *Journal des Inconnus*, she spotted a notice which caught her eye. It was an announcement for a conference which was to be held in Toledo, Ohio. Eunice had never been to Toledo. She tried vaguely to imagine what such a Spanish-sounding place in the Midwestern United States might look like --what she came up with was a distant view of tire factories by El Greco and dark women in mantillas eating at the counters of luncheonettes. The image intrigued her, and she resolved on the spot that she would go. She was after all on the editorial board of the *Inconnus*; she could probably swing an invitation, and her department would pay for the trip. She checked to see what topics were going to be covered by the conference. She was only momentarily daunted to read that the theme was Ukrainian Egg Painting of the Eighteenth Century. There would certainly be room for a comparative discussion of egg painting and dung sculpture. Completely forgetting the course which was scheduled to begin in forty minutes, she logged onto her computer and whipped off her proposal for this conference. The letter was a perfect balance of pleading and pressure.

With ten minutes to class time, she made a hasty call to the audio-visual library to see if they could come up with a film and a projector to replace today's lecture. Fortunately, Professor Severini had just shown *The Bicycle Thief*, a film Eunice knew to be artsy and had always wanted to see. So she had it brought over as a treat for her students, among whom she was extremely popular, above all for her spontaneity. She was on her way out the door when the phone rang.

"Professor Lattrey," she said impatiently. She hated to miss the beginning of a movie.

"Hello, Professor Lattrey. We just spoke a while ago about your book. There was one other question raised by the editor which we were hoping you could answer before it goes to press."

"Yes, what is it?" she said, simultaneously taking a final drag on her cigarette.

"Well, in Chapter Two, you describe the various methods of hardening the dung in order to make of it a more lasting medium. You criticize the technique of one tribe you encountered as being 'shitbrained'. The editor wanted to know -- "

"Print it!" interrupted Eunice, stomping out her cigarette in the over-full ashtray before her. If there was one thing this woman was proud of, it was her fearlessness in the face of controversy. She refused to euphemize. And besides, a little scandal might be good for sales and help her to recoup some of the losses incurred in bringing her ground-breaking research to light.

Magna ista scientarum mater

That great mother of sciences

Lakshme Phartah

Technician,

Department of Microbiology

Salary: $33,000

"**N**ow you're telling me that I am working for an undergraduate student?!" she protested, her stony, bug-eyed stare seemed to bore holes into her supervisor's skull.

"Well, I think that your wisdom and experience render you the best person to set an example and blaze the trail for students to follow. But, I leave it in your capable hands. You do as you think best." Professor Boyd quickly backed away, both literally and figuratively. He did not want to get involved in any internecine laboratory strife, least of all where Lakshme Phartah was concerned. His hasty departure for his other office, that of the Chairman of the Departments of Biological Sciences, left Lakshme once again reigning supreme in her position as Laboratory Queen.

One might assume from her attitude that Ms. Phartah was in fact a primary benefactor of the science departments at this university. From the way she spoke to other faculty, one might mistake her for at least a Full Professor, with her own laboratory. From the tone in which she delivered her edicts regarding laboratory protocols, one would be cowed into imagining that, Full Professor or not, she controlled her laboratory, both its administration and its scientific direction. In fact, and this was a source of infinite frustration to Lakshme, she was, and always had been, on the lowest rung of the scientific hierarchy, a mere technician with a Master's Degree from an Indian university, the very existence of which even other Indians questioned.

Every year she vowed to enter the Ph.D. program at this university. But her inordinate scientific responsibility to her research and her lab prevented her from carrying out the threat, which at this point no one took seriously. And her obligations, like her cell cultures, multiplied and were manifold. She alone had the all-important task of keeping each of the cell lines propagating. It was under the weight of this Responsibility that Lakshme dragged herself about the lab every day. Whereas, in most people, dedication -- to something, anything -- produced joy or at least some degree of gratification, for Lakshme it was a source of constant irritation and discontent. Her love for science, which had never been instinctive or profound, had thrust upon her a heavier yolk than any marriage or prison term, and she conducted herself accordingly. She took personally all laboratory problems, from the blowing of a light bulb in the cold room to the overheating of her growth medium in the autoclave.

With such extreme sensitivity to all functions of the lab, one might have assumed that Lakshme was a perfectionist in her work, and a great help to her colleagues. But no, when the light bulb blew, it was always somebody else's fault, when the beakers boiled over, somebody else had to clean up the mess. The daily difficulties of running a laboratory were grumpily noted by Lakshme, and were sarcastically commented upon by her, but they passed through her and were actually corrected by others.

If she took any pleasure at all in the laboratory, it was in satisfying her curiosity concerning the private lives of her co-workers. That, and watching accidents befall others, were the closest to diversions that Lakshme could afford, though in both cases, it must be said, the supreme pleasure came from reporting what she had learned or seen to her supervisor, Professor Boyd. This she considered to be the surest sign of her consummate professionalism.

While stirring the day's batch of cell culture medium, she thought again of the new undergraduate who was coming, and her knuckles whitened on the wand. Suddenly, the red dot dropped from her forehead and fell into the agar, causing her to shriek out an obscenity in Hindi. She made no attempt to retrieve it but hoped that the extreme temperature of the mixture would sterilize it, preventing it from endangering the cells. For the cells, as Professor Boyd had once remarked in her hearing, were like Lakshme's children, and she tended them with all the care of a true, many-handed goddess-mother.

As though she had conjured them up, Professor Boyd returned with his new advisee. After a very brief introduction he left the young woman to tour the laboratory with Lakshme. The latter eyed the newcomer critically and with undisguised scorn. She was blond. Lakshme hated all women, but blonds in particular. Furthermore, she was attractive, and overly friendly. There was no way that this woman was going to be allowed to interpose her curves and her kindness between the technician and her hard-edged, angular laboratory work.

Lakshme began in a monotone to describe the vital task she was performing, the focus of all her physical and intellectual energies, the stirring of the medium. After listening with interest, the undergraduate, whose name *would* be Debbie, actually interrupted to ask a question.

"Professor Boyd mentioned that you are in charge of preparing cells. So I guess I should just let you know when I will be needing them for my experiments?"

Lakshme looked as though she had been clubbed between the eyes, which rolled haphazardly in her head. With as much venom as she could inject into her tone, she snarled her reply.

"I am not paid thirty-six thousand dollars a year to handle the inane requests of students playing at being scientists."

Lakshme felt very strongly that her salary reflected her worth, as a scientist and as a person, rather than simply the length of time she had remained in this same job. It could be said that the major reason Lakshme had not prolonged, much less completed, her own graduate studies was so that she could claim to make more money than the graduate students and post-doctoral fellows around her.

When, after a pause, the girl responded, it was in a tone so deferential and apologetic that Lakshme recognized immediately her own good fortune. It would take months, perhaps a year, for this girl to realize that she had been doing Lakshme's work. And no doubt other unsuspecting undergraduates and graduate students who hoped to work with Professor Boyd would hear from this young woman of the technician's vast power and influence and intelligence and importance. And Lakshme, backed by her legions of cells, would continue to rule as Queen of the Lab.

De gustibus

Concerning tastes

Frank Larry

Assistant Professor,

Department of History

Salary: $30,000

You could not mistake the office of Professor Frank Larry, the latest addition to the History Department. On the door, above his name stenciled in spiky black with embossed studs, was a larger-than-life poster of a young man's naked backside with a baseball bat protruding from the cleft. At least it's the small end, thought most passers-by. And in fact, only a month after it had been taped up, the controversy had completely died down and nobody noticed it anymore.

From the athletic build of the boy in the blow-up, one was perhaps surprised to find out that behind the door lurked neither the stereotypical, hyper-masculine, biker-type homosexual, nor the equally stereotypical, flamboyant, effeminate kind. Instead, Professor Larry was a short, slightly flabby, thirty-four year old man, with lovely eyes and indifferent skin. He was, and this was the point, perfectly normal. But a few minutes in his office, and you would see that this semblance of normalcy was also misleading. For he was a missionary, and missionaries are, by their nature, zealots and extremists.

Today, Frank Larry was juggling several tasks, moving from file cabinet to telephone with a velocity and enthusiasm that belied his ovine shape. First, there were the final arrangements for his symposium, *Burn the Faggots: The Abuse of Homosexuals from Medieval to Modern Times.* At the last minute, three of his scheduled speakers had decided to back out. He was disconcerted by only one of the cancellations because he was sure that the other two were still heterosexuals. We say "still" because it was Professor Larry's deepest belief that all men were, or wanted to be, homosexual, and that, according to his research, it was only a matter of time before this fact was universally recognized. This, then, was his mission, to advance by his research and his own personal example the inevitable homosexualization of the world. The conservative university was to be his first challenge, and, given the number of uptight, closet queens he had already encountered in these two months, he was off to a promising start.

Aside from the symposium, he had to finalize and begin to circulate a petition denouncing a recent violation of gay rights by the administration. This had to do with the closure of all restrooms on campus after 11:30 PM. He hardly needed to explain how such an act slighted homosexuals and limited their freedoms. As the only place unaffected by the new rule was the gymnasium, did you have to be on the wrestling team to get it on with your classmates? And, if you were on the wrestling team, you were already getting it on with your classmates. Ditto for tennis. Would everyone eventually be driven back to playing "Smear the Queer"? Frank himself was determinedly anti-athletic, though he appreciated a tight jock strap as much as the next man.

Then there was the march against anti-gay graffiti, ominously on the rise in those very same restrooms which were now off-bounds to needy late-night visitors. Frank had been particularly offended by these unfeeling displays of homophobia, especially as there were several examples which referred specifically to him. For instance, one undergraduate had actually claimed, without the least embarrassment, to have recognized Professor Larry from a grotesque caricature he had seen in a popular lavatory at the Law School. And Frank himself had more than once been horrified to find, in the midst of exercising his God-given right to urinate in a seated position, mention of himself as "Fairy Larry" or "All Franks And No Beans". As a result, he was marshaling the extensive GLACK (Gay and Lesbian Activist Committee for Knowledge) forces in order to put a stop to this sort of abomination.

Like any other untenured faculty member, he also had classes to prepare. And he was conscientious about this, moreso than certain women (lesbians) he knew. It took him days to get into the right frame of mind to deliver a lecture such as *If This Bottom Could Talk: Famous Passives in American Political History.* And the grading alone for his hugely successful course on "Penis Imagery in Popular Culture" devoured a significant portion of every weekend. There was also the college-wide AIDS-awareness program to worry about; Professor Larry knew that if he did not maintain strict control of this well-funded project, someone like that old hag, Hannah Dartmouth, would get her claws into it and turn it into a vehicle for her own warped campaign against all forms of human intercourse, a campaign which was motivated by personal jealousy and reflected nothing other than her own sexual frustrations.

Finally, there was his research. It was all right for his dear friend, Eunice Lattrey, to publish shit, and to pay heavily for it, but Frank felt a greater responsibility to his followers and to himself. He had barely begun the transformation of his doctoral dissertation, on men's underwear, into book form, though, he considered with Pride, he had already been contacted by several publishers and offers of advance payments had been made.

In the midst of congratulating himself on his seriousness as a scholar, the telephone rang for the tenth time this afternoon. He groaned inwardly when he recognized the voice of Ruthita Clabber-Jones.

"Hi Ruthita. What is it now?" He made little attempt to be pleasant with her, his major rival in the contest for minority funding. And Ruthita was, as usual, deliberately stinging in her pretense at including Professor Larry in her vast Sisterhood.

"Frank, I've just heard that you and your girlfriends are planning to hold a symposium in Maxwell Hall auditorium on Saturday the eleventh? I think you should know that I've had that slot tentatively booked for some time. My meeting of Black Women in Black Business is an annual thing, and takes precedence. But I'm sure you'll find some other, smaller and more appropriate facilities for your get-together."

Frank made no further effort to conceal his irritation at this latest proof of the university's discriminatory -- or, more precisely, anti-gay -- policies.

"Fine, Ruthita," he said, his tone decidedly crisp. "We'll hold it in a big coat closet next door. Then you can attend both functions. After all, you'd be just the man to moderate our special session on Black transvestites."

With that, and without even pausing to enjoy his riposte, Professor Larry hung up the phone and once again threw himself into his work.

Semper fidelis

Ever faithful

Ramon Fernandez

Post-doctoral Fellow,

Department of Microbiology

Salary: $21,000

He obsessed over her, exposed himself, told her his secrets, actually showed her his prescription for Prozac.

Ramon Fernandez paced the cage-like cubbyhole which constituted his office space in Alvin Boyd's laboratory. It was only ten o'clock in the morning and he was already seething with anger at her delay. She would pay. He would make her pay. He would scream at her. He would call her names, new names that he hadn't used yet. He would rush at her, knock her down, make her bleed. Make her feel the pain she was causing him now.

When she finally arrived, at exactly the same time she arrived every morning, ten-fifteen, he pretended not to notice her for ten minutes. At last, restraining his anger, and with a great false smile which exposed his gritted teeth, he began the day's session. He accused her of keeping him waiting, not caring about his feelings, deliberately abusing him for her own enjoyment. Where had she been? Her eight-thirty English class lasted only an hour; that gave her forty-five minutes to cross the campus. He himself could do it in ten, but then, he was invariably running, chasing someone he thought might be her, or someone he hoped would be her, a phantom or a dream. And she always got away.

After the first few minutes of his tirade, she turned her head, undoubtedly ashamed of the way she treated him. But he knew she wasn't sincere. If she really loved him, she would cry, and beg for forgiveness. Nevertheless, he found himself pleading with her to have lunch with him, or even dinner, or coffee, or a candy bar in the lounge. And it filled him with rage when she told him simply she had work to do. He had work to do, too, but he was willing to make the sacrifice! After all, he was a post-doctoral fellow, and she was nothing but a spoiled and silly American undergraduate, whom Professor Boyd had placed under his supervision when the technician had tired of her and refused to continue the collaboration.

Debbie walked in the direction of her desk, and Ramon would have followed, except at that very moment, Alvin made one of his infrequent visits to the lab. A wave of bitterness coursed through the post-doctoral fellow's Costa Rican veins, when he recalled that His Debbie -- after all he had done for her, and all he had promised to do -- had complained to Alvin Boyd about what she felt was Ramon's harassment of her. Thank goodness Alvin had understood when Ramon explained that it was quite the opposite, that she had in fact been flirting with him from the start, and that she was the type of girl who clearly felt all men wanted her. He noted with some disgust that Alvin had stopped and was actually talking right now to His Debbie. If anybody was harassing her...

At eleven-fifteen, he was no longer able to stay in his cell. In the past hour, he had rearranged every item on his desk. He had checked three times to make sure that his photo of Debbie, taken by Professor Reuther at the recent departmental picnic, was still in its hallowed position in his top drawer. Finally, fretting madly about what His Debbie might be doing without him, he set off to find her, checking first to see that Alvin was not around. He felt as though his heart had been torn from his body when he noticed that she was not at her desk. Nor was she working at her lab bench. Nor in the coldroom. Nor in the supply closet. Nor in the stairwell. So he positioned himself outside of the women's restroom -- for fifteen whole minutes, during which time thoughts of where she might be dripped like icy water on his overheated brain. She must be avoiding him. To hurt him. To make him jealous. Good God! What if she had already gone to lunch?

At that moment, he saw red. He could hear, around the corner, the voice of His Debbie talking to a graduate student. A male graduate student. Her laugh reached Ramon where he stood outside the lavatory. How could she have betrayed him in this way? She was surely talking about him, slandering him, lying to her new "friend" and to herself as well. Maybe she was sleeping with him. He couldn't believe it. Tears filled his eyes. He walked past them heavily, feeling every one of his two-hundred and twenty pounds. He smiled at her lugubriously, and then, overcome by the sadness caused by her cruelty, he headed back to the lab, like the mourners he had seen at funerals in his native town.

Once at his desk, Ramon decided to call his wife, to share with her his anger and depression. His wife knew everything that Debbie had done to him, and Ramon gained strength from her hatred of the girl she had never seen, though he could not share that hatred. For Ramon would never stop loving Debbie, hoping that she might change her ways and realize her true feelings for him. He even forgave her, over and over again, for never giving in to him. He knew that she was only waiting, making him suffer, to increase his affection for her. She was not the first girl who had made him suffer; the last one had actually made it necessary for him to leave his appointment at another university. But Debbie was the most dangerous one so far. In his forty-one years, Ramon had never known such desire.

Ramon's wife was German, and took a far more clinical view of the situation than he did. His wife couldn't understand how he could tolerate Debbie's constant, aggressive pleas for his attention. She told him again that if this girl didn't leave him alone, he must register a formal complaint against her. But how could he risk getting His Debbie into trouble? Like most women, his wife was no help. When he hung up the phone he felt worse than before.

At one-thirty, Ramon was so hungry he could no longer wait for Debbie to come and ask him to accompany her for lunch. So he went to get her. She was sitting at her desk, eating the sandwich she had brought in a brown paper bag. As always, he was shocked and dismayed at her brutal lack of consideration. When he approached her she picked up her sandwich to leave the area, but he blocked her way. Though he had told her he was impotent -- in keeping with his Prozac story -- he could not hide his excitement. She looked as though she was about to scream when another post-doctoral fellow interrupted their intimate conversation by asking Debbie if she was all right. Was she sleeping with him, too? Ramon wondered. And the way she looked at him, her eyes constantly begging for more attention, companionship, love. He turned and walked away from them, overcome with emotion.

It took another two hours of frantic shuffling and rearranging at his desk for Ramon to regain his composure. He wept bitterly, uncontrollably, though he was careful to conceal his tears from his co-workers, the people who looked up to him for his manly stamina and his scientific prowess. But they and their admiration meant nothing to him compared to the love of His Debbie. Checking the copy of her schedule which he kept in his wallet, he realized with a start that her biology class ended at three-thirty. He raced out of the building in order to be waiting for her when she left the lecture hall. This time he circled the building repeatedly so as not to miss her if she should take the wrong exit.

Despite his precautions, he did not see her until she was already in the distance, hurrying toward her dormitory. In minutes he was at her side, protecting her. But he could not just forget her earlier cruelties, concerning which her silence now was a clear admission of guilt.

"...How could you do this to me? How could you sleep with all those other boys? Didn't I promise you I would leave my wife and child for you? Don't you believe me? Is it because of my problems? You're the only one who can help me. I need you! Didn't you know that I followed you last Friday when you went out with your other friends? I was sitting right behind you the whole time. I watched you eating. Doesn't that mean anything to you? Do you understand how you hurt me? I can't just let you walk out of my life! I need you! You are my life! My only reason for living. I would never let you go..."

Debbie was trying to open the door of her residence hall. Ramon was forcing it closed, confessing yet again his profound affection. After a few moments -- and still, as though instructed, without saying a word -- Debbie began to cry. Ramon rejoiced. Here was the proof he needed. He could now go on with his day. By her tears he knew that she owned him. He was, after all, Her Ramon.

Ave atque vale

Hail and farewell

Lola Severini

Assistant Professor,

Film Studies

Salary: $30,000

She wore what looked like a number of gorgeous, semi-transparent veils with no dress underneath. Her detractors, mostly women, said that she resembled a scarf-rack in an airport giftshop. Her admirers, mostly men, compared her to whatever their field of research made available to their minds: for Everett Morris in Ancient History, she was Salome; for Hans Reuther in his lab she was a perfect morphological match for the *Paramecium caudatum*, an analogy intended as the highest compliment to both specimens. American women would never try to get away with this, but part of Lola's success derived from her not being an American woman. And the rest of the secret lay in the fact that she didn't give a damn.

It was not about her students that she was uncaring. Nor about her scholarship, which meant more to her than anything except her husband and parents, and possibly her ancient hometown of Florence. It was for bureaucracy, and the boldfaced, unblinking idiocy of academic administrators, that Lola had no patience.

Now in her office, in the middle of preparing her course on Italian cinema, which she did meticulously, arranging the essential points in her lecture with the precision of a jeweler setting stones, she allowed her thoughts to wander momentarily to the upcoming meeting at which her tenure bid was to be decided. She had never dreamed, when she was young, that she would be a scholar, much less living in the United States and teaching at one of that country's most prestigious universities. Nor had she ever imagined that her future would be in the coarse and brutish hands of seven or eight overweight, middle-aged men and a smaller number of even more mannish women. Of course, the odds were against her, and that was not her fault, but due primarily to the fact that the subject of her research -- film history -- was outside the realm of the traditional academic disciplines. She herself belonged to no department at the university; the committee deciding whether or not to offer her a permanent contract was composed of faculty members from a variety of fields in the humanities, including Comparative Literature, with which she was nominally affiliated, English and the History of Art. Thus in the end, her fate was to be sealed by people who, like everybody else in the world, no doubt "liked movies," but had never treated them as worthy of serious study. And yet it was one of Lola's most heartfelt beliefs that if Giotto had lived in the twentieth century, he would have worked behind a movie camera, and if Ruskin had survived -- as it sometimes must have seemed he would -- into the nineteen fifties, he would have dumped Turner to write lengthy panegyrics on Laurence Olivier and the Ealing Studio comedies.

And even though, deep down, she didn't give a damn, Lola found herself hoping that she would succeed. She counted the people who had gone out of their way to offer her support. One of her strongest and most vocal allies was Hannah Dartmouth, who, at this very moment was, coincidentally, polishing her letter to the other members of Professor Severini's tenure committee. If, at this important juncture, we borrow a metaphor from film, and split the screen, in order to view both Lola in her office and Hannah across campus in hers, we will have the opportunity to glimpse a paragraph from the latter's statement regarding her younger colleague's prospects:

...I feel that it is my duty, both as a Woman and as a Scholar, to alert the committee to certain of Ms. Severini's character flaws. First and foremost, concerning her publication record: while it is true that Ms. Severini has published two books in a very short time, one with the highly respectable press which published my own groundbreaking *Miss- and Ms-ogeny*, this, rather than being impressive, should lead one to question the depth of her scholarship. To be thorough, I looked at Ms. Severini's eight-hundred page *World Cinema Between the Wars* and I must disagree vehemently with the popular reviews. To say nothing of the content, the length alone is utterly inappropriate to so obscure a topic. And why would a native Italian choose to write in English? Isn't she proud of her heritage? And why do her chapters on women in cinema constitute less than a quarter of the book, when women make up roughly half of the world's population?...

If we leave Professor Dartmouth to seal this letter, licking the envelope with a tongue that, if you believe her, once touched Sartre's, we can visit the office of another member of Lola Severini's tenure committee, Herbert Blake. Though his letter was also due by four o'clock this afternoon, Professor Blake was having far more difficulty than Professor Dartmouth in assessing Ms. Severini's achievements. Every time he began his summary, he became distracted by his ample recollections of her youth, her charisma, her lovely legs, her breasts, her eyes. These were not the qualities that he should be considering, much less emphasizing to the tenure committee, though there had been a time when they alone would have guaranteed her a permanent place in the university. But Herbert was too tired and too lazy to come up with new ways of describing Lola Severini's prodigious intelligence. And could she really be that intelligent if she had chosen to work in Film? Somebody had told him that she was the author of two lengthy and well-received studies of her subject. Herbert had had no time to read them -- in fact, he noticed with alarm, he was late right now. So with his usual resigned air, he wrote the standard, laudatory but not overly convincing, letter of approval. After all, he had bigger things to worry about than increasing the Mediterranean presence on campus.

Leaving Herbert to his trials, we might visit other members of the college community who have something to say about Lola Severini. For example, Donald Buchman, the Director of the University Art Museum and Adjunct Professor of Art History, might be seen dictating to his new secretary, Teesha Magruder, a beautifully phrased but vague and entirely meaningless series of comments reflecting less his familiarity with their ostensible subject, Ms. Severini, than the five martinis he had swallowed in quick succession at lunch. Moving down several rungs in the academic hierarchy, we might overhear two undergraduate students arguing over coffee in the library lounge, one violently defending Professor Severini as the best teacher she has ever had, the other, with equal violence, denouncing her as a symbol of the general decline in the quality of the university.

Finally, if we leave the controversy surrounding Ms. Severini's claims to a permanent position at this school, fast-forwarding the film of her life to the outcome of the debate, we find that Lola, unlike Eunice Lattrey, will not receive tenure, that within a year she will be forced to leave the university, that at the end of two years she will have her first child and that, shortly after becoming a mother, she will be appointed the head of the American Center for Film Study in New York, a position which will pay her twice her former salary as a teacher, though she will always look back fondly upon her days in the classroom.

Requiescat in pace

Rest in peace

Milton Burber

Full Professor, Chairman, Dean,

Department of Dramatic Arts and Theater Studies

Salary: $78,000

S ome students claimed that he had once been a Jesuit. Others, equally malicious, said that he wore a wig. There could be no doubt that he used cosmetics, for he left a light dusting of face powder whenever he remained in one place for any length of time. But really, was that so bad? Faculty wives defended him. After all, the Theater was his life.

It was a rare occasion when Professor Milton Burber, Founder, Chairman and Dean of the Dramatic Arts and Theater Studies Department, took it upon himself to direct an undergraduate production of a Great American Play. Those close to the sixtyish former child star of the New York stage, sensing that something momentous was in the works, had assumed -- and in some cases prayed -- that he was about to announce his retirement after over thirty years of service to the university. There was quite a stir when, instead of his departure, he informed his colleagues of his virtual return to a more active, "hands on", participation in the theatrical projects of his department.

His choice of *A Streetcar Named Desire* was at first lauded by the university community, both faculty and students alike. It was, after all, natural, as Professor Burber had known Tennessee Williams and had once succeeded in bringing the playwright to give a writing seminar at the school. That had been during Burber's heyday, following his transition from fading child actor on Broadway to blooming boy director of the energetic off-Broadway stage. It was at this moment that he had been snapped up by the university, as the only person in the Theater capable of single-handedly creating a Drama department worthy of the institution. Upon his arrival, he had shocked his unprepared employers by the flamboyance of both his person and his productions. However, to censure him would have seemed a retraction on their part, and an admission of their lack of wisdom. So they allowed him to continue his bawdy transformations of Euripides and Shakespeare, until finally, four years ago, after a nearly nude performance of Rostand's *Cyrano de Bergerac*, in which not only the nose but most of the title character's features were grotesquely enlarged, the President had, according to some, demanded Professor Burber's resignation. It was only after a vicious battle between the unpopular President and the Professor's lawyer that an agreement was reached; Burber retreated from the limelight but was officially promoted to a more responsible -- and more highly paid -- position as Drama Department Dean.

Three weeks ago, the president who had reprimanded Burber was found dead of heart failure in his bed. The next day, Professor Burber announced his resumption of an active role in university theater. And today were his first auditions for *Streetcar*.

Professor Burber appeared at the auditions in an outfit which made it clear that his banishment had in no way deflected his trajectory toward a sartorial apotheosis. The lines were normal enough, but the colors and textures were, by any standards, outlandish. Beneath a white, crepe de Chine jacket, his vest was a breastplate of silver peacock feathers, the shirt below was a deep shade of violet, and the bow tie was an unabashed orange. The trousers, pleated innumerable times in an attempt to camouflage his large and low-hanging waistline, were ash gray with a paler pin-stripe. The tongues of his Italian shoes were leopard skin, and there was a ribbon of the same material around his straw hat. Altogether, with the heavy makeup and -- whether it was a wig or not -- ill-fitting hair, he appeared like the discombobulated ghost of Diaghelev or some other deceased impresario who was told he had to make one more earthly appearance but wasn't given enough time to select a matching ensemble in the celestial fitting room.

After greeting his two assistants, Burber tapped his cane on the floor to bring the tryouts to order. The first name was called. A young man with blond hair and a big behind appeared. He was reading for the part of Stanley. When he was finished, Burber thanked him succinctly; though his assistants whispered their approval, the Dean said nothing more. The next hopeful was a slim, dark-haired, dark-eyed student of clear Mediterranean extraction. He, too, was reading for Stanley, and received exactly the same treatment as the blond. This scenario was repeated without alteration until the first female auditioner appeared. Her name was Marcia. When she was only half-way through reading for the part of Blanche, Burber himself interrupted her. What began as a mild admonition to please project more loudly, ended with the Professor shrieking for "Mar see ah" -- as he pronounced the girl's name -- to be so kind as to leave his presence.

At the end of the afternoon, the Dean was thoroughly exhausted and disgusted. The young men were, for the most part, tolerable, but the young women were appalling. And then, just as he was about to give up his dream altogether, it came to him, in the unquestionable, inexorable manner of all True Inspiration, the first he had experienced since his scandalous production of _Night of the Iguana_ in which all the actors had worn lizard suits of his own design. He would bring to the stage, at this piddling second-rate school, his all-male vision of _Streetcar_. Stella and Blanche would be what they had always been for Milton and Tennessee, brothers in cutoff jeans and tank-tops, fighting for the love of Stanley. It would be his tribute to the late president of the college, he would even have that printed in the programs, right underneath the words, in Gothic script, "Burber's Back."

Sic transit gloria mundi

So pass the glories of the world

Samuel Feldman

Horace B. Thrumboldt Professor of Biophysics

Salary: $78,000

I t was that time of day again. The hour of greatest disillusionment. He found himself in the same posture, in the same seat in fact, trying to keep his mind open, reminding himself that he was not alone, except in his all-encompassing intellect. For Samuel Feldman, Horace B. Thrumboldt Professor of Biophysics, bridged all gaps. He was a Renaissance man, an *homme de lettres* as well as a godson of Galileo, a man for all seasons, the man with a thousand hats. With his interdisciplinary background, with his unlimited intellectual interests, with his unbounded aspirations and his mastery of many fields, he was a human Byzantium, where all worlds met. And his character, like his physical appearance, was appropriately large and imposing. He knew the importance of being earnest, but was not blind to the folly of human wishes. A man of both sense and sensibility, he was no idiot, but a true man of the world. He had known hard times, far from the madding crowd, he had drunk deep from the golden bowl in the house of mirth. He was the Prophet, the Fountainhead, the Professor (of this last reference, to what is certainly the most obscure Bronte novel, he was especially proud, and it eased him in his present task).

Professor Feldman studied his shoes, they were black like everything else he wore. He delighted in the fact that people speculated on his reasons for wearing only this color. Some said he was imitating a black hole, some said he was in mourning for an imagined first wife or all the victims of the Holocaust, some assumed that he was trying to look artistic -- as though he needed to try! -- and avant garde. Others, more petty and negligible, whispered that he was merely hiding an excessive perspiration, or had chosen the color for its slimming effect. And the undergraduates universally agreed that whether or not this was his real motive, the clothing he wore reflected his empathy for the bad guy in Western films. The fact that he had provoked such debate was reason enough for Professor Feldman.

He heard the sound of a door opening, and the shuffling of several feet. Then he recognized the voices of Derek Renaud and Hans Reuther. Over the normal noises, he could hear their conversation, and it was exactly what Professor Feldman might have predicted. Hans was lamenting at some length the dearth of attractive females in the sciences, and Derek, chameleon that he was, had perfectly assimilated the tone of his older and more powerful colleague and was repeating the latter's ideas, altering only the phrasing, and even this in the most minimal way. Not that Reuther noticed, lost as he was in his dreams of rejuvenating his department -- and himself -- by recruiting some new blood. After a few minutes, they were gone.

The next thing to distract Professor Feldman was a pair of shoes other than his own. From their age and obvious cheapness, he knew they could only belong to Harold Lang. He looked upon Lang the way a world-famous violinist looks upon an old man playing the spoons; his feelings were one-half pity and one-half contempt. It was a mystery to Samuel how, if in fact there were beings higher than the human, of which he himself was a Remarkable Example, how could that greater force take responsibility for having created a Harold Lang? But this was not a mystery which preoccupied Professor Feldman for long because, following close upon the heels of Harold Lang, he recognized the unmistakable entrance of his own great nemesis in the sciences at this university, Max Stern.

The thought of Max Stern being so close at hand blocked the easy flow of Samuel Feldman's lofty thoughts. Moments ago he had been disposed to show mercy on even so limited a specimen as Harold Lang. Now his blood boiled and the broad expanse of his mind was overrun with murderous fancies. There should be separate facilities for named Professors, he thought to himself, for his title of Horace B. Thrumboldt Professor of Biophysics was almost the only official distinction which separated him from the likes of Stern. Both men were eagerly seeking the position of Dean of the Sciences, though only Samuel succeeded in concealing his eagerness. The very idea that he, Samuel Feldman, should be forced to compete with a mere scientist, one who had no knowledge of classical literature and who had never visited the art galleries of Greenwich Village or the Left Bank, left the more distinguished man straining to vent his bile. But here was hardly the place.

In a moment, muttering to himself about his own delusions of superiority, Max finished his business and left the room. In quick succession, his spot was taken by another, and really rather extraordinary pair of shoes. They were very expensive-looking, certainly Italian, with leopard-skin tongues. What Samuel noticed about them, aside from their unusual appearance, was the length of time they remained before him, as it seemed, glued to the floor.

And then, just as Professor Feldman was relaxing again, after the upset of the encounter with Stern, he was stunned to recognize, immediately next to him, the unmistakable feet of Margaret Fanshaw, shod as usual in thick leather loafers. But how could this be? The Decay of Western Civilization. Samuel could read the writing on the wall. (By the way, what was all this "Franks and Beans" business?) The fact that a woman, at least a woman of sorts, was actually occupying the neighboring stall, spurred Samuel on. With a great effort, and amid the sound of thunder, he discharged his final animosity toward an Imperfect World and fled without washing his hands.

Salus populi suprema est lex

The good of the people is supreme

Alvin Boyd

Full Professor, Department of Microbiology

Chairman, Departments of Biological Sciences

Salary: $88,000

"Oh hi Fanny," said Alvin cheerily, and from his tone you might have guessed that this telephone call from his colleague was the greatest compliment anyone had ever thought to pay the chairman. Without waiting for him to express further gratitude, Fanny was off and running.

"Listen, Boyd. If you don't get me more freezer space *maintenant*, I'm going to take over yours. You don't use it anyway, what with your chair*manly* duties preventing you from doing any real research."

"Now Fanny, that's not fair!" Chairman Boyd responded, chuckling, though at the same time he was rubbing his forehead anxiously, cursing the ill fortune that had led him without thinking to respond to his own telephone.

"Fair shmair," snapped Fanny. With the funding she had, she knew she could trample anybody she liked, including the Chair.

"Well, Fanny, I think we can do something for you. As a matter of fact, I've already spoken to Hans. But to be perfectly democratic about it, you'll have to give up something in return." Alvin simultaneously jotted a note to himself to call Hans Reuther as soon as he was through with Fanny. "For example, you could --"

But at the thought of relinquishing anything, Fanny bolted. "No deals, Boyd. And if you can't get me that space, I'm sure the next chairman will." And she hung up the phone.

Alvin was momentarily daunted by Fanny's suggestion that he might be replaced as chairman. Such a turn of events would force him back into his laboratory, which had become, since his taking on the administrative control of the department, a foreign place peopled by unusual and unfriendly creatures. As if to illustrate this dark thought, Alvin noticed that his technician, Lakshme Phartah, was straining her neck towards his door in order to gather any small pieces of useful information which might help her in subduing more ignorant members of the staff. The simplest solution to his new problem with Fanny would be to grant her some of his own freezer space, which she had in any case threatened to take, but this alternative would require him to lock horns with Lakshme, who was very protective of all laboratory equipment. So he began dialing phone numbers furiously, and finally reached Hans Reuther in his dark room.

"Hans!" Alvin began, as though saluting his boyhood friend. "I've got a favor to ask you. Fanny's bucking for more freezer space, and since all of your work is with warm-blooded organisms, I was hoping that you might --"

Now it was Hans's turn to interrupt. This was a golden opportunity for the microscopist.

"Alvin! I was going to call you. Do you still have that undergraduate intern, Didi or something? You know, the one whose photograph is in this year's departmental brochure?"

"Oh, you mean Debbie? A pretty, blond girl?" Alvin knew instantly where his colleague was heading. "I'm afraid we had to hand her over to Lucretia. There was a personality conflict with one of my post-doctoral fellows."

"Oh but I love people with strong personalities!" Hans said gleefully. A complicated psyche, especially when reflected in the loveliest of female faces, was exactly the type of companion Hans needed to break up the monotony of his dark-room rituals. "And she would be my only intern, so there couldn't be any more problems like the one you describe."

"Yes, I see, and I'd be glad to try and convince Lucretia to send her to you for a few days each week, or to have her transferred altogether." Alvin was forced to raise his voice over the din of a number of large Pyrex beakers breaking in succession. Lakshme.

"Well if you can obtain that assistant for me," Hans continued, anxious to avoid any first-hand exchange with Lucretia, "You can do whatever you like with my freezer space. You know how I like to be a team player."

Both men liked to be team players, which is why Alvin immediately called Lucretia after hanging up with Hans.

"Lucretia! It's Alvin."

"Who? Look, I'm a very busy woman --"

"It's Alvin Boyd, your Chairman." Alvin pretended to be amused, just in case Lucretia was only pretending not to recognize him.

"Well, I'm still a very busy woman, so make it quick," Lucretia responded in the same unsentimental tone.

"I was wondering. You remember the undergraduate I sent you a little while ago? Debbie? How is that working out?" Alvin circled the issue so as not to give up his hand; after all, it would be disastrous if his colleagues were to strike a deal that didn't include him.

"Yes, I remember her. She's working out fine. Except that your Puerto Rican post-doc keeps popping into my lab, interfering with her work and getting in my way."

This information about Ramon -- for it must be Ramon, as he was the closest thing to a Puerto Rican in Alvin's lab -- disturbed the latter. It contradicted his previous assumption, based on Ramon's own account of the unpleasant situation, that Debbie was aggressively distracting Ramon with her advances. But his overriding priority now was to find that freezer space for Fanny.

"Well I think I can solve that problem for you. If you could find a project for her which requires some electron microscopy, you could send her to Reuther once or twice a week, and then you'd have both her and Ramon out of your hair."

Lucretia was automatically suspicious of this proposal. She thought Boyd must be up to his usual tricks. She instantly turned the tables on him.

"What a good idea! I'll call Hans right away and see if he agrees."

Alvin almost passed out at this suggestion. "No! I mean, I've already talked to Hans. You see I was naturally worried about Didi's welfare. After all, she was originally my responsibility."

Lucretia paused, thinking what she might demand as a reward for participating in Boyd's obvious plan. She had nearly everything she wanted. Ah, there was one thing.

"Okay, Alvin. I'll let you have Debbie back, if you help me. There's a funny little man coming up for tenure soon, no doubt you know who I mean. Shrimpton. Yes, yes, I know he's thought to be very good. But I know better. The man's got to go. I've rounded up a few abstentions, but a definite 'no' vote from the two of us would carry a great deal of weight."

Alvin thought for a moment. It seemed a minor request. Shrimpton was young and single. He would have no trouble finding another job, given the success of his recent work. It was a glimpse of Ramon, looking even more lugubrious than usual as he paced the lab, which finally frightened Professor Boyd into a definitive agreement with Lucretia.

"Why it's amazing how often we see eye to eye, Lucretia," Alvin responded, adding with unwonted flirtatiousness, "we ought to join forces more often." And each of them hung up the phone, delighted with this latest proof of departmental solidarity.

Ars lunga, vita brevis
Art long, life short

Donald Buchman

Director, University Art Museum

Adjunct Professor, Department of Art History

Salary: $85,000

With one step left to go, Donald Buchman rested. The swift descent from his office left him rather dizzy, and the pause provided him with his favorite view of the courtyard of his museum, where over a hundred people were already milling about -- a fine representative sampling of the regular attendance. And Donald was, naturally, one step above them all.

And to what did he owe this superiority? To many things, to his profound wit, to his wide reading and his cosmopolitan background, and above all to the fact that he was neither fish nor fowl, he was neither an academic, strictly speaking, nor a businessman, but brought with him the best of both worlds in fulfilling his position as University Art Museum Director. It was not that Donald Buchman did not pay a price for his exalted status. To begin with, he was fatter than was healthy, and most people felt he looked far older than his forty-six years. But these were necessary side effects of the socializing he was forced to do, both within and without the University -- the long lunches, the official dinners, the receptions, such as the one this evening, at which the alcohol flowed so freely that it seemed to lap at the heels of the people standing about as on a beach when the tide comes in.

Trying vainly to shake off his drunkenness from lunch before diving in again tonight, Donald took the last step and suddenly found himself among Them. And who were They? The usual academic art gallery reception rabble. There were the few bookish students actually looking at the pictures, which in the present exhibition consisted of thirty or so small photographs representing extreme close-up views of the female genitalia, though they might also, alternatively, have been details of the insides of flowers or seashells; hence the variety of intellectual responses to be heard from those students ("How vaginal they seem." or else "How strangely floral, or like a seashell.") There were the students who considered it jejune to look at the pictures, at least during the reception, and their saying so constituted another of the most frequently heard comments. Then there were the adults, whom Donald identified -- whether they were known to him or not -- as belonging to one of three categories. First of all were the Important People, people of power in the university or people with money who had given or might be talked into giving Something Tangible to the University Museum. Secondly were the Standards, a large group comprising less significant members of the university community, the lonelier element among the faculty, single men who couldn't prepare their own meals and consequently turned up for the catered food, the less wealthy and more pretentious sector of the general public, and the various unlikely creatures who made up Mr. Buchman's museum staff. Finally, on the last rung, were the Negligibles, the people with no real reason for being there except to create embarrassment or a conversational diversion for the other two groups, individuals who seemed to have wandered in off the streets, and for the removal of whom the police had more than once been roused.

Though he could not honestly recall obtaining it, Donald found himself with an unmixed drink in his hand, which was actually very fortunate considering the first person who cornered him. This was Gloria Faver, his Assistant Director.

"You know," Gloria chimed, tugging with some urgency at her employer's elbow, and nearly causing him to spill his drink, which he preferred for a number of reasons not to do, "the lighting isn't very successful after all. The jewel-like quality of the photographs is lost."

This was an absolute lie. Donald had overseen the lighting himself, and his taste was faultless. He studied his second-in-command; she was short, round and, in her characteristic formless black dress, resembled nothing so much as a sack of charcoal briquets. Or better still, with her big bob of dark hair, her large bosom and her low-slung hips, she looked like three big black beads on a string. The woman was notorious for flatulence in her office and other, more obvious forms of cruelty to her underlings. And she was after Donald's job. But despite all of this, he could not imagine finding anyone more ideally suited to take the flack for his unpopular decisions and his thankfully rare errors of judgment. The lighting of the present exhibition was not one of the latter, but the director smilingly avenged himself upon his assistant by answering her criticism with a pair of lies which shut her up immediately, and sent her off to fetch another drink.

"I couldn't agree with you more. I'll have it changed tomorrow."

With Gloria out of the way, Donald was able to relax into his second drink, in the company of his old friend, Whit Buttrey. The Buttreys were big benefactors, not only of the museum, but of the University as a whole. In this, Whit and his two brothers continued a tradition which went back uncountable -- and of course uncorrupted -- generations, to the just-after-the-Mayflower bondsman who founded the family fortune. The tradition can be summarized very succinctly as a reciprocal arrangement between all Buttreys and the University, according to which every male Buttrey was granted an undergraduate degree, an intellectual feat invariably celebrated by a substantial increase in the family's endowment to the college. This applied regardless of the actual worthiness of the Buttrey male, or for that matter of the university; there was even the case of Cotton Buttrey, who had died in infancy in the early nineteenth century but who was all the same awarded a diploma _in absentia_, a sentimental act which resulted in a new wing for (what was now known as) the old library.

"Hey old man," said Whit, lightly whacking the Museum Director on his corduroy-jacketed right arm.

"Hey there," responded Donald, keeping a slight distance, because although he was genuinely fond of the Buttrey brothers, he did not want to be spat upon, and Whit was the worst of them all when it came to moistness of lip and looseness of tongue.

"I've just inherited a lot of old Chinese stuff from my aunt, and I'd like the museum to have a look at it. If there's anything you want, it's yours." And as Whit said this, Donald was relieved to see the expected shower fall in the empty space between them.

"Great news," responded the Director, with his usual nonchalance. "I'll let Hermione know."

Both men automatically scanned the room, to see if the Curator of Asian Art was present, and, if so, to make sure that she was not in their immediate vicinity. For Hermione Vane was among the most boring and indefatigable conversationalists on the Museum staff.

At last Donald spotted her, the unmistakable craquelure of her complexion belying her claim to be "not quite fifty," at a comfortable distance.

"Tell me, Donald," Whit continued, once he too had sighted Professor Vane, "is it true that she's actually straight? I mean, I always thought she was a lesbian."

Donald laughed out loud, the deep, manly laugh that always accompanied his fourth drink. "If she's straight, then I'm Queen Christina of Sweden!"

It was for lines like this that Donald was famous -- words and phrases that proved the breadth and depth of his knowledge, colorful expressions that were invariably metaphorical and passed as the hallmark of urbanity, or else precise and historical, showing his razor intellect and infallible memory. Whit had never heard of Queen Christina, but he laughed wholeheartedly along with Donald at this latest example of the latter's wit.

"Well, I'd better go chat up some less generous old boys," said Donald, smiling and turning back towards the bar.

"Sure thing," sprayed Whit. "Oh, by the way, I hope you and Lucy can make it next week to the University Theater. Whit the fourth is starring in a play. I know the boy'd be pleased to see you there."

"What play is that?" asked Donald, already moving away.

"A Streetcar Named Desire," answered the proud father. "He hasn't told us much about it, but I assume he's playing the lead."

The voice of Whit Buttrey died in Donald's ears; the Director was in circulation again. He stopped to flatter several old women, whose clothes he recognized as those of spinsters with money, and one young one, Dixie Maxwell, a student whose voice and demeanor irritated him but whose father was on the Museum Board. At the bar for his seventh drink, he bumped into Gloria again, and made a note to find out from his other staff members whether she had a drinking problem. Then, when the crowd reached its peak in terms of size, Donald began to loosen up. He started to throw his arms around some of the Important People, a gesture which was received differently depending upon the individual so honored. From a corner of the courtyard, Gloria, morose in her own alcohol-induced stupor, was nevertheless conscious of her boss's every move. After his eighteenth drink, when most of the guests had gone, Donald grabbed one of the few coats remaining in the cloakroom and headed wearily to his car.

An hour later, still on his way back to Lucy and a house filled with paintings by and from grateful living artists whose work he had shown in the museum, Donald suffered from the strange delusion that he was driving the wrong way on a one-way street. But that couldn't be true. He tried to concentrate more on the road and less on the reception, memories of which seemed to flash across his windshield. Had he really insulted one of the deans? Is it possible that he had stuck his tongue deep into the bartender's undergraduate ear? Had he deliberately tripped Gloria as she wove her way back to the ladies room? Had the police been called this time?

But he relaxed. That was his job. There was his house. This was his life.

Quo vadis?

Where are you going?

Mark Frye

Associate Professor,

Department of Cellular Biology

Salary: $53,000

Mark Frye was forty-two years old, of medium height, of medium build -- all things considered, a medium individual. By profession a molecular biologist, he had come to this University from Industry and had been an Assistant Professor here for eighteen months, after which time he had decided to return to Industry. This was actually the third time he had fled from an academic institution back into the ever-forgiving, maternal arms of Free Enterprise. For this reason, Mark would have preferred to go quietly, rather than being feted with the farewell party at which he was now forced to appear.

Between sips of beer or wine, nearly every person in the large conference room glanced surreptitiously at the guest of honor. It would have been difficult for an outside observer to determine whether the occasion being celebrated inside the room was happy or sad. Even moreso than at other parties, that depended upon the individual:

Max Stern, engrossed in a heated conversation with "Fanny" Fanshaw, took only a quick look at Frye. Who did this so-called professional think he was? Stern could not believe that the various departments of scientific research at this University had actually stooped to notice the disgraceful and untimely departure of so Unworthy a Person. Of course, Max had been favorably impressed by Frye when he was first recruited, and had wholeheartedly supported his hiring, considering himself the Savior of yet another scientist from the purgatorial grip of Industry. But Frye's departure after only a year and a half was farcical, and Max intended to make a point of criticizing such behavior at the next faculty meeting, where his speech on the subject would confound all irresponsible activity with general immorality and even the subversion of scientific progress. This demonstration of his courage to speak out in the face of adversity would be sure to guarantee his overwhelming election as the new Dean of the Sciences. The thought of his imminent victory made his eyes swim with tears.

Professor Fanshaw noticed nothing of Max's lachrymal secretions, which ought, for professional reasons, to have interested her. She was far too busy describing to Max her own troubles with other faculty members and various departmental allocations, for example, the freezer space which she was preparing to steal from Alvin Boyd. Mark Frye's departure meant only one thing to her: his laboratory would soon be up for grabs. She considered ambling over to him and asking him for his keys. At the idea, she tossed her thick mane of auburn-tinted hair, and took one step backward, causing her to stomp on the foot of Harold Lang, an accident for which it would never have crossed her mind to apologize.

Harold Lang, however, apologized immediately. Then he went back to studying young Professor Frye. It was hard for Harold not to think of the man's departure as an escape from the increasing pressures of academic research. He knew that Professor Frye had failed to garner sufficient funds for his laboratory, and he assumed that this was the reason for his short stay in Academia. Harold himself had once considered moving to Industry, but at that very time the undergraduates had voted him the University's Outstanding Teacher, a privilege which had caused him no little shame for having even considered abandoning his true, albeit psychologically exacting, vocation. On his way out the door, he paused to congratulate Michael Shrimpton on his new baby.

Shrimpton paused in the middle of trying to swallow an *hors d'oeuvre* larger than his mouth and acknowledged Harold's little speech with a nod. This, according to Professor Shrimpton's automatic pilot, was the required response to a person of Harold Lang's professional status and political power within the University. Then Shrimpton turned back to his interlocutor, a female graduate student whose name he couldn't recall. Neither Shrimpton nor his new friend seemed to have the least idea of what this reception was for. They merely continued munching and chatting, ostensibly about their respective departments but actually about their own prospects in the scientific world. It was not until ten or fifteen minutes had passed that Shrimpton wondered to himself how on earth Harold Lang had heard about his new baby, as he had made it a point to keep the details of his personal life a secret from his colleagues.

Hovering about this unnamed graduate student was a man who found her extremely attractive, and regretted that he had ultimately decided not to bring his camera in order to record Professor Frye's final professional appearance at the University. When Hans Reuther had first arrived at the party, he had been somewhat envious of his departing colleague's prospects in his new position. The higher salary, the high turnover of secretaries, the yearly recruiting of young females fresh out of school. Then his eyes happened to light upon Shrimpton's companion, and his spirits were lifted. She was not unlike his new undergraduate intern, Debbie, whom he had tried to convince to accompany him to this event. But the girl had gently -- and, come to think of it, really rather playfully -- removed his hand from around her waist and, under the red light of the darkroom, claimed that she had homework to do.

And hovering about Hans was Ramon Fernandez. Ramon was typically depressed, this time due to the absence of His Debbie. When he congratulated Professor Frye on his new position, he noted that Frye, too, seemed sad. Had this man also slept with His Debbie? Ramon was left to wonder.

Studiously avoiding Ramon, in fact studiously avoiding everyone from his own laboratory, was Alvin Boyd. After a difficult week, he was still chairman, and this fact alone gave him cause to celebrate. And now, with Mark Frye leaving, there would be all sorts of expensive equipment to auction off to his colleagues. Not to mention the opening of a new position which would allow him to bargain with departments at other universities. This thought was so exhilarating that he forgot altogether to read his perfunctory farewell speech, a fact which Samuel Feldman noted with disgust.

Though Professor Feldman had no use for Mark Frye, since the young man had once failed to guess the source of an obscure poem he had quoted, he still felt that the chairman's sloppy etiquette in neglecting to fulfill his formal duties at occasions such as this indicated the general decline of the University. He would decry the chairman's failings at the next administrative meeting, rousing his audience to a general denunciation of any member of the faculty who dared to violate the time-honored policies and traditions of the scientific community, traditions which -- he knew better than anyone -- went back to the age of Aristotle. In his mind Samuel envisioned his oration and the subsequent reaction which would ensure his appointment as Dean of the Sciences.

In the very center of the room stood Professor, soon to be merely Doctor, Frye. He was extremely sad. And it was not because three of the five members of his laboratory staff had boycotted the reception, and would soon be forced to find work elsewhere. Nor was it because he was saying good-bye. He had been through all of that before. He surveyed the room, watching his colleagues from varying distances. For each face there was a very good reason for leaving academia. But in the middle of congratulating himself on his decision, he suddenly remembered the reasons he had left Industry. And they were the same.

Op. cit.

Everett Morris

Wilfrid F. Thrush Professor of Ancient History

Salary: $75,000

I t was Everett Morris's favorite time of day. The light of late afternoon wound its way languidly through the maze of trees, and shook its golden shower against the window of Everett's office on the top floor of Buttrey Tower. Everett looked up to greet the gilded rain, as Danae might have welcomed Zeus. [3]

Professor Morris removed his spectacles, and gently massaged his tired eyes. He was hard at work as usual. There were twelve essays from his seminar to correct, like the Twelve Labors of Hercules,[4] thought Everett. And there was his article to write for the festschrift of his old friend, Leopold Maypole, who was finally retiring from the University of ------. Everett was truly exhausted, but then that came with the job. He recalled the occasion upon which he had first been appointed the Wilfrid F. Thrush Professor of Ancient History; a delegation from the Dean's office had come to him and, with tears in his eyes, he had answered their proposal in the words of Augustus, "I have at last achieved my highest ambition."[5] But the fulfillment of that ambition demanded so much in terms of time and, yes, even emotional commitment.

He shifted his considerable bulk in the swivel chair and ran fingers knotted by decades of pen-pushing through his damp, silver hair. Despite his legendary calm, Everett was in a constant sweat --

---

[3]Ovid ?
[4]The Labours of Hercules, as first illustrated in the temple of Zeus at Olympia.
[5]Suetonius, *The Twelve Caeesers*, II, 58.

but, he liked to remind himself, the same had been true of Alexander.[6]
He opened the first essay, by one of the best Classics majors he had
ever come across, a young man named Simon Billet. He pored over the
text, occasionally circling a word in pencil, and at the end writing,
"Keep up the good work, B+". Then he turned back to the second page
of the essay (which was, by the way, on expressions of betrayal and
self-betrayal in the plays of Sophocles). Opening his own notebook, he
jotted down a few of Mr. Billet's references, and then moved on to the
next essay, by a lesser light in the seminar, Sarah Powell. From her
performance, entitled, "Betrayal and Self-Betrayal in Aeschylus: Plays
and Fragments," Professor Morris found it necessary to copy only one
fairly uninteresting comment, and even that he was forced to check
against the original source. Her paper received what he considered a
very generous "C-".

When Professor Morris had read and graded eight of the
twelve student papers from his seminar, he had already gathered a
sufficient number of references and suggestions to write his own article
for the festschrift, which he intended to call, "Betrayal and Self-
Betrayal in Greek Drama: A Revisionist Overview." That he had
assigned subsidiary topics to his pupils, far from causing Everett
twinges of conscience, seemed to him the most natural thing in the
world. In fact, he no longer thought of it, since he had first adopted the
ingenious practice and established it as a personal tradition some
twenty-five years ago. Consequently, his own article for Leopold
Maypole, a man for whom he had almost no professional respect and
against whom he had waged many battles in print -- battles invariably
arising from different interpretations of obscure usages in minor Latin
poems -- would be drawn, like the Helen of Zeuxis, from a variety of
sources,[7] and would, like her, be a worthier and more beautiful
contribution thereby.

But, though the greater part of his work was finished, four
essays remained to be read. Not wishing, like Odysseus, to delay his
journey home any longer than was necessary, he spread all four out on
his desk, planning to skim two pages of each as quickly as possible, and
then, on the basis of this limited reading, to grade them and be gone.
But on the first page of the second essay, he came upon a passage
which made him, like Belshazzar,[8] tremble with helpless rage. The
opening paragraph of the essay, written by a fairly stupid but

---

[6]Plutarch, *Lives of Illustrious Men*, Alexander.
[7]Pliny the Elder, *Natural History*,
[8]Daniel 5:25

ostentatiously wealthy student named Neil Prescott, bore a distinct resemblance to the second paragraph in the paper by Simon Billet. Professor Morris reeled. He felt, before the treachery of this Prescott, exactly as Hipponax of Ephesus must have felt, in the presence of Boupalos,[9] or Phocylides of Miletus faced with an unnamed antagonist.[10] It was some moments before the possibility dawned upon Everett that Mr. Prescott may not have been the plagiarist, or at least not the sole plagiarist. And as he pondered these alternatives, he grew more and more convinced that he himself had recognized the passage upon first reading it -- that its original appeal had been in part the result of this vague sense of familiarity.

With the sun setting beyond the trees below his window, Everett began rifling through the books and files that lined the walls of his vast office. And at last, with his overworked heart fluttering madly, he found what he was looking for, an essay "On Retribution in the Dramas of Sophocles," published in a long-forgotten collection of articles by none other than his old rival, Leopold Maypole!

After the initial shock, after his ire had somewhat abated, Everett Morris laughed. But his indignation remained. Professor Morris, like Callimachus, loathed all vulgar things,[11] and cheating was vulgar. He decided instantly that both students would be brought up before the Committee on Academic Integrity, of which he had long been a member. He sat down to write an official letter to the Committee, and then, remembering that nearly ten years ago a similar incident had occurred in a course taught by one of his colleagues, he was actually able to locate the letter the colleague had written to the Committee, and what is more, he found it enormously timesaving in writing his own.

After reading the last three student papers with exceptional care, Everett packed up his briefcase, and prepared to leave for home. When he had turned off the light, he paused, as always, and reflected upon a day's work well done. He was tired, but wiser, and is not wisdom, as Plato says, one of the most beautiful of things?[12] And if there was little beyond his office, out there, where the trees no longer cast their shadows, is not each man's life sufficient?[13]

---

[9]_Anthologia Lyrica Graeca_, Hipponax, 70 (Diehl)
[10]ibid., Phocylides, 1 (Diehl)
[11]Callimachus, _Epigrams_, XXX
[12]Plato, _Symposium_, 204d
[13]Marcus Aurelius, _Meditations_, II, 6

Quidquid agas, prudenter agas et respice finem

Whatever you do, do cautiously and look to the end

Albert Bloomsburg

Visiting Associate Professor,

Department of Biochemistry

Salary: $48,000

"I am Professor Albert Bloomsburg, Visiting Scholar in the Department of Biochemistry." He said no more, but stared at the woman as though, with the revelation of his identity, she would fall prostrate at his feet.

The librarian considered her position for a moment and then repeated, without blinking, that Visiting Professor Bloomsburg was not entitled to check out materials for indefinite periods.

At this inconceivable attack on his prestige and his divine right to special privileges wherever he went, Professor Bloomsburg, Visiting Scholar and self-proclaimed Scientific Great, let his books fall to the counter, pursed his lips viperously and seemed prepared to lunge at his ignorant persecutor. When, after a moment of suspense, he opened his mouth, the sound he emitted was surprisingly musical, though his meaning was no less stinging for that.

"My dear Madam, it is highly regrettable that you have thus abused your insignificant position in preventing me, Albert Bloomsburg, Visiting Scholar, from carrying out my responsibilities to my students. In refusing me these obscure books, all of which happen to have been written by very dear friends of mine, you have denied me the resources for sufficiently preparing my courses, an act which, I am sure, the Administration will seek to avenge. In short, I expect that, if and when I am so unfortunate as to meet you again, I will be carrying these same books and you will be carrying a tin cup outside the library door."

The librarian, known on campus as Kindly Old Mrs. Pendergras, watched the Visiting Scholar take his leave. She had not heard a word he had said, but she remained extremely impressed by his tone. She assumed he was English from his voice, but in this, as opposed to her knowledge of the library's lending regulations, she was mistaken. Professor Bloomsburg, Visiting Scholar, was in fact Canadian. It is true that, fifteen years ago, he had been accepted into a year-long program of study in London as an undergraduate, but he had been so miserable there that he had returned to Ontario before the year was up. Nevertheless, from this period, he had adopted an English accent, which became more pronounced as time went by. Though any Englishman would have seen through his affectation, most Americans -- remember that American academics are notoriously Anglophilic -- were only too happy to welcome him as the Real Thing and flatter themselves with his attention. Mrs. Pendergras actually felt honored to have had her little conversation with him, and described in some detail the Visiting Scholar, rather than her own defense of library policy, to her colleagues behind the desk.

Meanwhile, Professor Bloomsburg, Visiting Scholar, marched across campus in a rage. He had graced this university for only three weeks and he already found it almost unbearable. He felt patronized by his peers -- who pretended to listen to, but basically ignored, him -- spied upon by the graduate students -- who seemed all too eager to claim his insights as their own -- and pressured by the undergraduates -- who claimed as *their* right all of his precious time. When he had applied for this position, he had believed that it would be a relaxing opportunity to do his own research, a kind of sabbatical which would, at the same time, be a highly respectable addition to his *curriculum vitae*. But that was not the way things were turning out. To his dismay, the courses he had been assigned were not simply senior tutorials, which demanded no preparation on his part and could be combined with an occasional lunch at the expense of the department. Rather, they included two introductory lecture courses with huge numbers of students, and he himself had not looked over the material since his own undergraduate days. With all the bitterness of the Unrecognized Genius, he entered his painfully tight office space and began to read a copy of the latest issue of *Biophysica*. After barely two minutes there was a knock at the door.

"Excuse me," said a young undergraduate female, opening the door before the Visiting Scholar had time to hide beneath his desk.

"What do you want?" he snapped even more angrily than usual, for in his fumbled attempt to conceal himself he had knelt on a staple.

"Well, Professor Bloomsburg, I am a little confused about what you said in the last lecture about the Ideal Gas Law --"

"I am sorry," he interrupted her, "but perhaps you are unaware that, as a Visiting Scholar, I am not required to hold office hours, nor to answer questions that are more efficiently handled by your textbook." With that, he stood up as though to dismiss the girl.

"But it was because of an ambiguity in the textbook that I've come --" she pleaded.

Visiting Scholar Bloomsburg turned his back to the girl and looked out the window. It seemed as though she were pursuing him and these were the bars of his cage. "I don't have time for this nonsense." The Ideal Gas Law was not his strong point.

"I have tried to get ahold of the teaching assistants but they don't seem to understand the text either. One suggested I come to see you."

This was too much. As though driven there by years of frustration, Visiting Professor Bloomsburg leaned against the long window, which he never bothered to fasten. It gave way before him. Shoddy Americans, was his final thought, as he fell three floors to the flagstones below and died.

And thus Albert Bloomsburg's Visit came to an untimely end.

Cum finis est licitus, etiam media sunt licita

So the end justifies the means

Stuart Kneebling

Professor Emeritus,

Department of Romance Languages

Salary: $41,000

Bickering with the ghosts of long-dead colleagues, the walking remains of Stuart Kneebling, Professor Emeritus of French Literature, were often to be seen wandering the dark corridors of Maxwell Hall by jumpy, first-year undergraduates who, encountering the guttering sockets and the ashen skin and the mouth which looked as though it had been sewn up to prevent his spirit from escaping, invariably asked the impressive personage if he needed help, and even when he had assured them impatiently that he was fine, still walked away considering that they ought to telephone security, though in fact the only assistance Professor Kneebling required was in locating the door of the office which he had successfully, and against considerable territorial encroachments, guarded as his own for over fifty-three uninterrupted and, on the whole, uneventful years.

Sicut erat in principio

This is our sense of it

Custodial Epilogue

On the underside of the hill, hidden among blasted trees at the end of a small avenue of dumpsters, the outdoor, industrial furnace glowed beneath a moonless sky, like the forge of Vulcan, like a witches' bonfire from the painted nightmares of Salvator Rosa. The light of this fire cast an appropriately lurid gleam upon the faces of two old friends who met there every night, Joe and Joe. Joe was a tall, heavyset black man with obvious dental irregularities, while Joe was a shorter but equally thick Pole, with a pitted face. Though both appeared lighthearted and casual, they were quite serious about the nightly ritual in which they were engaged.

Joe, having dragged a large bag of garbage nearer the mouth of the fire, was slowly feeding its contents to the flames, when he stopped to lift and exhibit an immense handful of candy wrappers, even more than usual.

"Professor Lopez," Joe chuckled, and tossed the foil wrappers into the smoking maw.

On the other side of the fire, Joe raised his gloved hand and produced, as though magically out of the night air, an expensive long-sleeved shirt and tie, both speckled with food particles.

"Mr. Swallow," Joe pronounced, with a proud glance at his companion, for he knew that this put him in the lead.

Meanwhile Joe was drawing a seemingly endless number of glass shards from his bag. It was his habit to overwhelm with quantity. But the broken beakers were not his real treasure. He topped it with a stack of unfinished letters, each in the same hand, each bearing the same salute to "My Dearest Debbie."

"Alvin Boyd and Co." And he dropped the letters into the furnace, one at a time. Now they were even.

Not to be so easily cowed, Joe showed great delicacy in retrieving his next discovery, a small black figurine carved from some unknown material, with odd shells and feathers pressed into its surface. In the shape of a man, it was missing one of its arms and a portion of its head.

"Professor Lattrey." And into the blaze it went, along with an enormous number of cigarette butts.

At this point, Joe produced a clotted ball of crusted cloth, and a sheaf of underexposed photographs, a horde which he referred to in its entirety as "Professor Reuther". Like a seasoned gambler, Joe countered with another trump, the contents of a wastebasket from Dean Burber's office bathroom, complete with hairpins, lipstick tubes, face-powder containers and discolored puffs.

In the dark, the avenue of dumpsters looked like rows of buildings, and the two friends illuminated by the blaze, like Atlantes, like destructive gods in a picture by Goya. This game went on for hours, but the end was always the same.

Sint ut sunt aut non sint

Let them be as they are or not be

-- Pope Clement XIII